IMAGES
of Sports

RUNNIN' RAMS
UNIVERSITY OF RHODE ISLAND
BASKETBALL

RHODE ISLAND BASKETBALL WITH A LOCAL FLAVOR. In the first half of the 20th century, most Rhode Island State College players were from New England, many from Rhode Island. This 1946–1947 Rhody team won 17 games and lost 3. The starters, from left to right, are Ken Goodwin (Somerville, Massachusetts), Al Palmieri (New Bedford, Massachusetts), Sal Sclafani (New Rochelle, New York), Dick Hole (Newport, Rhode Island), and Jackie Allen (Newport, Rhode Island).

IMAGES
of Sports

RUNNIN' RAMS
UNIVERSITY OF RHODE ISLAND
BASKETBALL

William Woodward

ARCADIA

First printed in 2002.

Published by Arcadia Publishing,
an imprint of Tempus Publishing, Inc.
2A Cumberland Street
Charleston, SC 29401

Printed in Great Britain.

Library of Congress Catalog Card Number: 2002106715

For all general information contact Arcadia Publishing at:
Telephone 843-853-2070
Fax 843-853-0044
E-Mail sales@arcadiapublishing.com

For customer service and orders:
Toll-Free 1-888-313-2665

Visit us on the internet at http://www.arcadiapublishing.com

"IF YOU DON'T LOVE TO WIN, PIVOT AND GO HOME!" Rhody's legendary coach Frank
Keaney gives his 1940–1941 team some preseason advice. He enjoyed inventing colorful impact
words and phrases. A chemistry professor and coach of football, basketball, and baseball, he was
known as the "Menty" to his players and students. The above advice apparently worked as the
team went on to a 21–4 season, including the Rams' first postseason appearance.

CONTENTS

ACKNOWLEDGMENTS

In writing this pictorial history I have been blessed with a remarkable team of supporters for whom I am most grateful. I am deeply indebted to David Maslyn and Serena Wyant of the University of Rhode Island Library Special Collections for their untiring effort and cooperation in helping with research material and pictorial searches. Their belief in this project and their trust in allowing me access to the wealth of archival resources are greatly appreciated.

The support and assistance of the URI Athletic Media Relations Office greatly enhanced my work. I thank Mike Ballweg, director of sports information, and his staff—Dan Booth, George Nonis, and Eliott Tannenbaum—all of whom greeted me warmly on my many intrusions and assisted me in a host of ways. I wish to thank Jennifer Silva, my student intern assistant, for her efficient help with the logistical challenges of creating this pictorial history.

I am grateful to Ron Petro, director of athletics, and Robert Beagle, vice-president of University Development, for inviting me to do this history of University of Rhode Island basketball and for giving me their support and encouragement. My thanks also go to various URI alumni and staff whose assistance in identifications and suggestions have helped assure the book's authenticity and accuracy. I thank Robert Pickard and Nora Lewis of the URI Publications Office for their cordial welcomes and helpful advice. I appreciate the assistance of Michele Nota, director of URI Alumni Relations, and Paul Whitney, director of the URI Bookstore. I extend special thanks to Tiffany Howe and Amy Sutton of Arcadia Publishing.

My gratitude goes to Ernie Calverley for sharing his rich memories and treasure of scrapbooks and memorabilia. I thank Carl Koussa for his wealth of knowledge about decades of URI basketball, and for sharing his special collection of photographs. I wish to thank Michael Delany and his pleasant and knowledgeable staff at the Providence Journal Visuals Division for their assistance. I wish to note the cooperation of Kingstown Camera in Wakefield, Rhode Island, with special thanks to staff member Marsha Goldstein, URI Class of 1973, for her courtesy and professionalism.

Finally, I thank my devoted wife, Grace for her constant encouragement and her patience with a preoccupied husband. Fortunately, she is a great Rhody basketball fan and has been on my side since the opening jump ball.

—William Woodward

All photographs, unless otherwise noted, are courtesy of the University of Rhode Island Library Special Collections and Archives or the URI Athletic Media Relations Office. The cover photograph is by Nora Lewis.

This book is dedicated to all University of Rhode Island
student-athletes who have been privileged to wear
the Rhody Runnin' Rams basketball uniform.

INTRODUCTION

In December 1891, the game of basketball was invented by Dr. James Naismith at the Springfield, Massachusetts, YMCA. Several months later, in 1892, the institution that eventually became the University of Rhode Island was given college status by the state legislators. The coincidental infancies of the game and the college evolved into a unique relationship. The college influenced the game, and the game influenced the college.

This historical account of 100 years of University of Rhode Island basketball portrays the importance of the game of basketball to student body spirit, alumni enthusiasm, and state pride. Basketball became the centerpiece of campus life and helped lift the college to national prominence. The story also tells how an ingenious, feisty, and creative teacher-coach, Frank W. Keaney, changed the game of basketball during its adolescent years from a stodgy, slow-tempo game with little scoring to a firehorse style of play with lots of scoring. His innovations of the fast-break offense and the full-court press defense were initially met with derision by the so-called experts, but he eventually gained favor with basketball aficionados. His up-tempo and spirited manner of play helped nurture a love for the game on the Kingston campus, throughout the state, and eventually throughout the country.

Keaney's teams became the showpiece of New England basketball during the 1930s, when the boys in blue led the nation in team scoring averages for nine of those ten years. The team became known as "the two-points-per-minute Rams," numbers never expected by the good Dr. Naismith when he first hung his peach basket on the wall of the Springfield YMCA. He and Keaney became good friends during the 1930s. Naismith was pleased with the influence that Keaney was having on his game.

Rhode Island went on to national prominence in the 1940s, when Keaney and his teams invaded Madison Square Garden, the mecca of college basketball, and won the hearts of sophisticated fans and a skeptical press with their entertaining style of play. The Rams became the darlings of New York and made four appearances in the National Invitation Tournament (NIT) between 1941 and 1946, coming within one point of winning a national title in the 1946 final against Adolph Rupp's University of Kentucky Wildcats.

Following Keaney's retirement, Rhode Island's succeeding teams added to the tradition of exciting basketball on the Kingston campus. A new state-of-the-art gymnasium, named in Keaney's honor, opened in 1953. The Naismith Memorial Basketball Hall of Fame recognized Keaney for his contributions to the game as one of its earliest inductees in 1960.

Rhode Island's teams of the 1950s, 1960s, and 1970s had varying levels of success. Playing in the newly formed Yankee Conference, comprised of the six New England land grant state universities, the Rams engaged in annual battles for supremacy with their longtime archrival, the University of Connecticut (UConn) Huskies. The record books reveal that many excellent players, drawn by a desire to play URI's traditional up-tempo brand of ball, found their way to Kingston to play for the Runnin' Rams. Although postseason play was infrequent, National Collegiate Athletic Association (NCAA) bids came in 1961 and 1966.

In the 1970s, Rhode Island women's basketball gained full varsity status and garnered its own faithful following. The program grew to a high level, with some outstanding players and several winning seasons in the 1980s. An NCAA bid finally was earned in 1996. The program has continued to grow with a solid base of fans from all corners of the university community.

The men's program returned to consistent national prominence in the 1980s and 1990s, achieving four NIT bids and six NCAA appearances from 1978 to 1999. In 1982, the Rams joined the newly formed Atlantic 10 Conference, comprised of eastern colleges with rich basketball traditions. The Atlantic 10 has consistently been among the leading power conferences in the country. The 1987–1988 team reached the Sweet Sixteen round of the NCAA, and the 1997–1998 team came within seconds of a Final Four appearance. A solid number of Ram stars achieved innumerable records, gained conference and national awards, and several moved on to successful professional playing careers.

The tradition of excellence and excitement has been sustained. The Thomas M. Ryan Convocation Center, opened in 2002, is the new home for men's and women's basketball at the University of Rhode Island. With a seating capacity of 8,000, it will host another century of success for the Runnin' Rams.

This unique relationship between the game and the college results in an intriguing and exciting story. Along with highlighting Rhody's great teams, players, and coaches, this pictorial history also portrays the exciting environment in which they have played their games. May this walk through time enhance your understanding and appreciation for the rich tradition of Rhode Island Ram basketball.

LET'S GO, RHODY! The players are being introduced. The coaches are prepared. The band is ready. Rhody the Ram is raring to go, and the crowd is in a fervor. It is time for University of Rhode Island Runnin' Rams basketball.

One

A NEW GAME—A NEW COLLEGE
1902–1920

LIPPITT HALL—RHODE ISLAND BASKETBALL'S FIRST HOME. Lippitt Hall was built in 1897 and was the home court for Rhode Island basketball until 1928. A drill hall–gymnasium was located on the top floor, above a chapel and library. The building, which still stands on the college's main quadrangle, was named for Charles W. Lippitt, the governor of Rhode Island, "in appreciation for his support given to the enterprise" and, as some hoped, for his continued support of the new college. The first record of the new gym's use for basketball is in the 1899 yearbook: "We have an outfit for playing basket ball, but the girls are the only ones who have an opportunity to play; for during the only hours which boys have for playing, the faculty or the Grange hold their meetings in the chapel underneath, and we are not allowed to play such a noisy game, because we disturb the meetings. We will not kick, however, but will accept with thankfulness the few crumbs which fall to our lot."

THE 1903–1904 GIRLS' TEAM. Early basketball teams for the coeds were called girls' teams. The first girls' team (1901–1902) actually preceded the initial boys' team by two years. Pictured here is the 1903–1904 team. Sometimes the college's early teams included female faculty members. The few games that were played were typically among campus groups and friends. During the early years, there is record of an occasional intercollegiate game, mainly with Pembroke, Brown's sister school.

THE 1903–1904 BOYS' FRESHMAN TEAM. The college's Boys Athletic Association officially recognized basketball for the 1903–1904 season. There was no coach, and only four games were played—all against high schools. A 2-2 record was achieved. The next year there was no team. In the fall of 1905, P.H. Wessels, a chemist in the Agricultural Experiment Station, was named coach. He selected a team of all-stars following the intramural playoffs. The first ever intercollegiate game was played against the University of New Hampshire, with Rhode Island winning 26-20.

10

RHODE ISLAND STATE'S 1906–1907 BOYS' TEAM. Coach P.H. Wessels's second team, 1906–1907, was the college's first to play a majority of intercollegiate opponents, including the first contest with the University of Connecticut—a 23-18 win in New London. The season was cut short by two games; Massachusetts State and Brown University canceled "for diverse reasons. Brown Varsity did not deign to answer any communications."

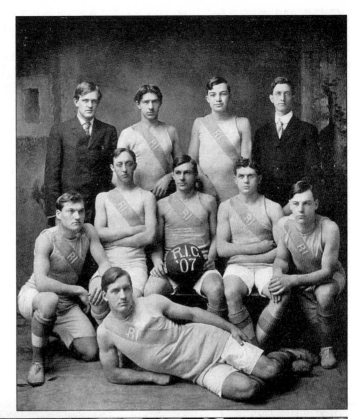

LIPPITT HALL'S HOME COURT ADVANTAGE. In its early years, Lippitt Hall's gym, on the top floor, was considered to be as fine a facility of its kind as any in New England. In addition to basketball games, it was used for proms, drills, intramurals, and general college gatherings. Here it is decorated for the Sophomore Hop. For basketball games, spectators stood along the sidewalls or the end baselines.

THE 1909–1910 GIRLS' TEAM.
The first ever home-and-home series was played against Brown University by this girls' team of 1909–1910. In Providence, Brown won 22-3. Apparently, there was considerable confusion on the part of the Rhody girls concerning sidelines and different rules. The second game was played in Kingston and resulted in a 10–7 victory. Bertha Nutting "threw" four baskets and Electra Cobb had one. There is evidence that home teams were able to amend rules, perhaps giving early meaning to the concept of home court advantage.

THE 1912–1913 TEAM. In 1912, basketball was pronounced "the strongest branch of athletics" at the college. Nonetheless, scheduling difficulties and a lack of money caused the college to drop the sport from 1913 to 1915. Harold Browning (back left), the assistant student manager, had a long career as an educator at his alma mater, eventually serving as a distinguished dean and vice-president of the college. He oversaw a Rhode Island basketball program that attained national prominence.

12

"SULLY" (1909–1913) AND TULLY (1912–1915), RHODY'S FIRST STAR PLAYERS. The "Basketball Song," probably the college's first ever sports song, gives a glimpse of how the young game of basketball and its star players started to capture the fancy of the student body. It was is sung to the tune of "What's the Matter with Father." Verses two and three reveal a special affection for John Sullivan (above) and William Tully (left).

    Basketball Song
  What's the matter with Sully?
  He's all right!
  What's the matter with Tully?
  He's all right!
  Captain Neal can play the game,
  Trout and Beany are just the same.
  What's the matter with the whole team?
  They're all right!

  What's the matter with Sully?
  He is fast!
  What's the matter with Sully?
  He can pass!
  He's the wizard at basketball,
  He's got something on them all.
  Oh, what's the matter with Sully?
  He's got class!

COACH JIM BALDWIN'S FIRST TEAM, 1915–1916. Basketball returned to the campus in the fall of 1916 and lived precariously for the next few years with the war raging in Europe. Collegiate athletics, never vigorous, were cut back by declining enrollments. Jim Baldwin's reign as coach lasted three years. His replacement, Fred Walker, lasted six months, and his successor was Fred Murray, who stayed for one year. The women's program was limited to interclass and intramural play. Verse one of the "Basketball Song" revealed the lingering hopes for basketball's stability and success.

>   Basketball Song
> What's the matter with Rhody?
> She's all right!
> What's the matter with Rhody?
> She can fight!
> She trimmed Trinity, Tech, and Maine,
> And New Hampshire got the same.
> Oh, what's the matter with Rhody?
> She's all right!

Little did the lyricist know that what lay ahead for the Rhode Island State basketball was going to be well beyond "all right."

Two
The Keaney Era
1920–1948

Frank William Keaney. In 1920, the college secured a coach who brought instant credibility and ultimate fame to the athletic program. Frank William Keaney was hired as the head coach of football, basketball, baseball, track, and cross-country—a literal one man athletic department. He served as athletic director for 36 years In addition, he taught chemistry for 15 years. He embodied the scholar-athlete ideal. He was a philosopher scientist, mathematician, linguist, and literary expert. He employed these disciplines in lessons taught on the field , court and track. His infectious demeanor appealed to his student-athletes and the faculty. He was a baseball genius and football innovator, but basketball was his centerpiece, the sport that catapulted Rhode Island to national prominence.

KEANEY'S FIRST TEAM, 1920–1921. Frank Keaney (back right) poses with his first Rhode Island team on the steps of Lippitt Hall. The opening game was played at home against Providence College, the first ever against the Friars. Providence was defeated by a score of 87-25. This prodigious point output was unheard of and proved to be an omen for Rhode Island basketball. Keaney led his team to a 9-8 record. The next season was his only losing season (7 wins and 8 losses).

WINIFRED KEANEY. When Frank Keaney was hired, the college received an unexpected bonus for women student-athletes: his wife, Winifred Keaney (back right). The two met at Bates College, where Winifred excelled in athletics. Like her husband, she had special gifts for successful coaching. Here, she poses with her 1924–1925 team. By 1930, her teams were playing a full intercollegiate schedule.

16

A NEW HOME FOR BASKETBALL. As Frank Keaney infused the student body, faculty, and townspeople with a growing passion for college basketball, a new home for the Rams was needed. In 1928, this new gymnasium and armory was opened, serving the men's basketball team and the Reserve Officers Training Corps (ROTC). The seating capacity was 1,400, though it was noted that "Keaney's systematic way of seating the crowd" increased the capacity to 1,832. It is here that Keaney revolutionized the game. The building is known as the "cradle of the fast break."

THOMAS C. RODMAN. In 1938, the college named the gymnasium-armory in honor of Thomas C. Rodman, a widely respected gentleman who was a member of the college's first faculty. He was an instructor of wood and iron works and later served as the supervisor of buildings.

THE FIRST POINT-A-MINUTE TEAM, 1932–1933. During the 1930s, Rhode Island State College basketball teams led the nation in average points per game in nine of the ten years. This 1932–1933 team achieved a 14-4 win-loss record, including two wins each over Brown University and the University of Connecticut, and was the first to achieve a point-a-minute average. By the end of the decade they were dubbed the "two-points-per-minute Rams."

FRANK "HAP" APPLIN—RHODY'S FIRST "BIG MAN." The early 1930s brought an unusual sight to the Kingston campus: a six-foot eight-inch basketball player strolling about. Frank Applin, appropriately nicknamed "Hap" because of his chronic smile, was a force at his center position. He helped lead the Rams to a 39-13 record from 1932 to 1935. With the center jump after each basket in place until 1935, Hap proved to be a great weapon. In the spring he was Frank Keaney's first baseman on the baseball diamond.

VARSITY BASKETBALL TEAM WINS 14 OUT OF 18 GAMES

Freshman Quintet Has Fine Record; Don...

STATE FIVE DOWNS CONN. AGGIES 41-29

Cox, Kilroy, Horseman and Donovan Star in Roughly Played Game.

R. I. State Quintet Rallies to Defeat Pratt Team 41-36

Applin, Speckman and Marty-nik Collect Nine Successive Points at End.

TECH FIVE DEFEATS R. I. STATE 40-33

Coaches Wre...

Rams Top Huskies 38 to 37 After Trailing at Half-Time

Second Half Rally Brings Kea-... Five Victory.—State ...in 49-38.

College Sport Results

R. I. STATE TOPS NUTMEGGERS 41-34

Connecticut Athletes Take Three of Five Events on Day's Sports Program.

RAM FIVE WINS OVER GOBS 38-32

STATE FIVE LOSES TO BROOKLYN TEAM

Visitors Stage Fast Passing ...k in Second Half to

STATE QUINTET WHIPS BROWN 44-23

Rams Topple Arnold Quintet 50 to 38 For Second Victory

Horseman Leads State to Triumph by Scoring 16 Points.

STATE FIVE BEATS WORCESTER TECH

Rams Score 18 Successive Points in Final Minutes.

Ramlets Win, 57-33.

Cox Leads State's Scoring Attack, Tallies 18 Points

1300 See Game at Kingston; Ramlets Subdue Bear Cubs 48-28.

Rhode Island State Five Beats Brown to Make Clean Sweep of Series

State 'Varsity Five Ga... Early Lead and Hold to the End; Four Pl... Banished on Fouls

CRIMSON "INDIES" WIN OVER STAT... QUINTET

Woodruff Leads Colle... uates to Brilliant Vic... with 13 Points.

RAMS TOP ST. MICHAEL'S FIVE IN ROUGH GAME

STATE SWAMPS FITCHBURG 63-...

Rams; Fresh... 66-21.

COAST GUARD FIVE TOPS STATE TEAM

Cadets Also Win Fencing Match But Lose in Wrestling and Shooting.

R. I. STATE FIVE DOWNS TEACHERS

STATE FIVE DOWNS PANZER 44 TO 42

R. I. State Victorious Over Northeastern Five 37-32

Rams Take Eight-Point Lead in First Half; Ramlets Are Beaten 36-33

BASKETBALL FEVER IN THE 1930s. A string of very successful seasons, coupled with Frank Keaney's colorful demeanor and contagious enthusiasm for teaching and playing the game, brought capacity crowds to Rodman Hall throughout the 1930s. Fans queued up hours before each game, and as the doors opened, they made their mad dash to get the best seats. To meet the demands for tickets, the athletic department eventually had to divide its ducat distribution to half of the student body for every other game. It became common for both students and faculty to attend Keaney's practices, which were always open. The coach loved a stage. The students loved their Rams. The faculty loved great teaching. Keaney became known affectionately as the Menty—testament to his creative ways of teaching his lessons—on the court, in the classroom, or during an informal stroll across the campus. Keaney's joyful, high energy, and flamboyant demeanor gave great life and spirit to the campus, even as the nation was struggling to recover from the Great Depression.

BASKETBALL HALL OF FAMER WILLIAM MOKRAY. William Mokray graduated from Rhode Island State College in 1929 and shortly thereafter became the college's sports information and publicity director. He is credited with giving Rhody teams the name Rams. He promoted Keaney's firehorse style of basketball. Mokray left Rhode Island for the Boston Celtics, where he served as vice president and the director of the Boston Garden. He was the founder and editor of the *Official NBA Guide*. His stature as the foremost basketball historian of his time led to his 1965 induction into the Naismith Memorial Basketball Hall of Fame.

MOKRAY'S "BIBLE" ON THE RAMS. In 1940, Bill Mokray wrote about Frank Keaney's two-points-per-minute offense and distributed it to the sports press corps across the nation. It was designed to give the Rams national exposure, and it inspired numerous columns about the coach and his fast break. This is the cover of the 16-page booklet.

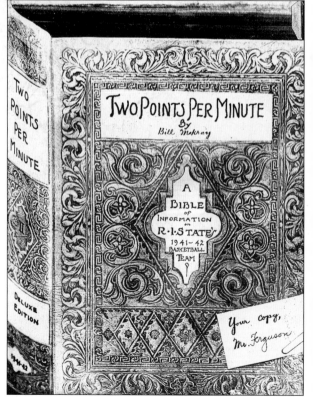

THE 1936–1937 STARTING FIVE.
The 1936–1937 team was Rhode Island's winningest team to date, with 18 victories in their 21 games. The starters, from left to right, are Jim Wright, Art Tashjian, Jack Messina, Chet Jaworski, and Morris Fabricant. Jaworski, a sophomore in this photograph, became one of the country's top players. In the 1937–1938 season, he led the nation in average scoring with 22.6 points per game and was named Rhode Island's first All-American. (Courtesy Providence Journal.)

RHODY'S STARTING FIVE, 1938–1939. This 1938–1939 team won its first 13 games, extending the Rams' overall win streak to 22. Pictured here, from left to right, are the formidable first five: Warner Keaney, Leon Caprielian, Chet Jaworski (captain), Fred "Bud" Conley, and Ed Petro. Jaworski scored 1,426 career points and is 23rd on the all-time scoring list. Conley was a prolific scorer as well, giving the Rams a superb one-two punch. He scored 1,395 points and is 25th on the all-time list. The team won 17 games and lost 4.

21

LIKE FATHER, LIKE SON. Coach Keaney (right) had two sons, Frank Jr. and Warner (left). Both played football, basketball, and baseball on their father's teams. Frank Keaney Jr., Class of 1936, distinguished himself as an outstanding punter on the first football team to beat intrastate rival Brown University (1935). He became a war hero, serving as a B-24 navigator on regular bombing missions over Austria and Italy. He had a distinguished career as a secondary school teacher, coach, and counselor. Warner Keaney, Class of 1941, starred in all three sports. Imposing in size—6 feet 4 inches tall, weighing 270 pounds—he had remarkable agility and noteworthy arm strength. He played quarterback in football and pitched in baseball. He featured this throwing ability in basketball, as he cleared defensive rebounds and quickly unleashed half to full-court passes, on a line, to teammates fast-breaking toward the basket. When Rhody made its first visit to Madison Square Garden in January 1941, Warner dazzled the appreciative New York fans with his awesome rebounding and strong passes. He was also an excellent free throw shooter. He went on to a highly successful career as a coach of football, basketball, and baseball at South Kingstown High School in nearby Wakefield, just three miles from the college campus.

PACKING THEM INTO RODMAN. Here is the unique seating pattern of the Rams' home gymnasium. Fans would queue up hours before game time on cold winter nights with the hope of attaining choice seats along the balcony rails, where legs dangled over the court, greatly distracting the visiting players during warmups. Joe Paterno, legendary Penn State football coach, once played in Rodman while at Brown University, and recalls "great memories of playing basketball in Rodman Hall, the greatest snake pit ever."

THE "BIG SIX" OF 1940–1941. The Rams' remarkable success during the 1930s blossomed into even greater heights in the 1940s. The 1940–1941 team was the first to win 20 games, the first to play in Madison Square Garden, and the first to be invited to the National Invitational Tournament (NIT), the prestige event of the time. The "Big Six," from left to right, are Bob Applebee, Billy Rutledge, Bud Conley, Warner Keaney, Stutz Modzelewski, and Earl Shannon.

23

STANLEY "STUTZ" MODZELEWSKI. In 1938, Stanley "Stutz" Modzelewski arrived in Kingston. He was destined to become a three-time All-American and set a national career scoring record, amassing 1,730 points (currently 10th all-time for Rhode Island). He could score from anywhere and, with his speed and quickness was perfect for Keaney's fast break. Modzelewski scorched the nets for 40 points in a 102-81 win over the University of Connecticut in March 1940, a New England Conference record at the time. He played for the New York Knicks and eventually became an National Basketball Association (NBA) referee.

STUTZ'S LEARNING DEVICE. This unusual photograph shows Stutz Modzelewski comparing a basketball with a toy rubber ball. As a boy growing up in Worcester, Massachusetts, he practiced throwing small balls into tin cans. It paid off, as he eventually became the national scoring leader playing for Rhode Island State College. He was nicknamed Stutz because of his love for the Stutz Bearcat automobile. After college, he changed his last name from Modzelewski to Stutz.

RHODY FANS VISIT MADISON SQUARE GARDEN. On January 29, 1941, the highflying Rams made their first visit to Madison Square Garden and became instant favorites. The Garden trip became an annual event and started a new tradition, a reserved train called the "Rhody Special" that left from the Kingston Station loaded with rabid fans. In the front, from left to right, students Dave Hedison, George Martin, and Frank Cromwell are rooting Rhody to an overtime Garden victory over Fordham in January 1942.

KEANEY AS AN INVENTOR. Coach Keaney's innovative approach to coaching did not stop with technique and strategy. He invented this Keaney rim, an insert rim two inches less in diameter than regulation, to increase his players' concentration during shooting practice. In a small chemistry lab in his Rodman office he concocted special liniments for athlete's foot, soreness, blisters, and itches, and he developed the Keaney blue color to make his teams look distinctive. To prepare his team for the smoky environment of Madison Square Garden, he placed smudge pots in Rodman during practice sessions.

DURING THE HECTIC BROWN UNIVERSITY GAME, MARCH 1942. To date, Brown University and Rhode Island have played each other 143 times. Rhode Island has won 91, and Brown 52. This 1942 photograph was taken in Brown's Marvel Gym when the underdog Bears upset Rhody 83-82. It was the Rams' last regular season game, and it was feared that the loss might cost them a coveted NIT bid. Happily, good news came the next day from the tournament committee.

STUTZ ON TOP OF THE BASKETBALL WORLD. Frank Lanning served the Providence Journal as its sports cartoonist over a period of five decades. Here is his rendering of Stanley "Stutz" Modzelewski after his collegiate career ended in 1942 with a total of 1,730 points, a national record at that time. Modzelewski had been named an All-American as a sophomore, junior, and senior.

THE SLENDER SNIPER FROM PAWTUCKET. World War II took its toll on the college's athletic program, but basketball survived. The schedule was limited to New England teams and included a large number of contests against U.S. military establishments. The roster was limited to young men who had deferred induction status with the military. Ernie Calverley, a 17-year-old who had been an All-State and All-New England player for Pawtucket East High School, arrived in Kingston in the fall of 1942. Freshmen were eligible to play varsity during the war, and Calverley immediately made an impact, scoring 346 points and leading the Rams to a 16-3 season. Although he was only 5 feet 10 inches tall and weighed about 130 pounds, he was a dazzling ball handler and great shooter who had speed, poise, and steadiness. In the spring of 1943, Uncle Sam came calling, and Ernie served five months in the Army Air Corps. A subsequent physical exam revealed a heart murmur, and Ernie was discharged. He returned to college, uncertain about his future as an athlete, but was able to respond to the rigors of basketball and captained the Rams for three seasons. He led his team in scoring each year, ultimately breaking the national career scoring record with 1,868 points, and was twice named All-American. His four Rhode Island teams won 71 games and lost only 17.

PATHE NEWS FILMS *BASKET WIZARDS*. As the war raged in both the European and Pacific theaters, home-front efforts to boost the morale of the troops took on many dimensions. In December 1943, Pathe News, noted for current news films in local theaters throughout the country, produced the exciting story of Rhode Island State College basketball and Frank Keaney's fast break in a special 10-minute film, *Basket Wizards*, which was distributed abroad as entertainment for U.S. servicemen and servicewomen.

THE 1944–1945 STARTING FIVE. As the war wound down, some sense of normalcy returned to the Kingston campus. The Rams concluded the 1944–1945 season with 20 wins and 5 losses, ringing up 100 points 5 times. The NIT came calling, and Rhode Island defeated the Tennessee Volunteers in the opening round but were overwhelmed in the semifinals against De Paul University, the nation's number one team, led by six-foot ten-inch All-American George Mikan. From left to right are Dick Hole, Ernie Calverley, Frank Keaney, Bob Shea, Al Nichols, and Mike Santoro.

THREE RHODE ISLANDERS WITH LOTS OF POINTS. The three leading scorers for the 1944–1945 Rams were all former Rhode Island schoolboy stars. Their point numbers tell the continuing story of Rhody's high-octane offense. From left to right are Dick Hole from Newport, Ernie Calverley from Pawtucket, and Mike Santoro from Westerly. (Courtesy Providence Journal.)

THE 1945–1946 TEAM DESTINED FOR GREATNESS. Following V-J Day in August 1945, campus life burst forth with great activity. A joyful winter for Rhode Island basketball fans lay ahead. The Rams won 21 and lost 3, received an NIT bid to fill the sterling field of eight, and reached the final game before succumbing to the Kentucky Wildcats by one point in a national championship game. Above, from left to right, are Bob Shea, Al Palmieri, Sal Sclafani, Dick Hole, Al Nichols, Jackie Allen, and Ernie Calverley.

THE SHOT HEARD 'ROUND THE WORLD. At the end of the first-round game in the 1946 NIT at Madison Square Garden, Ernie Calverley is carried off the floor after thrilling the crowd with one of the greatest moments in collegiate basketball history. Pitted against heavily favored Bowling Green University, led by six-foot eleven-inch All-American center Don Otten, Rhody was down 74-72 with three seconds to go and had the ball in the backcourt. Receiving a pass in bounds from Bob Shea, Calverley let go with a mighty 62-foot shot that swished through the net as time ran out, forcing overtime. Pandemonium broke loose. In the extra period, the Rams gained the lead and Calverley deftly dribbled all over the court, controlling the ball and putting the finishing touches on Rhody's greatest victory, 82-79. Rhode Island advanced to the semifinals to face Muhlenberg College. Other tournament teams were Kentucky, West Virginia, St. John's, Arizona, and Syracuse. (Associated Press photograph, courtesy Providence Journal.)

MARTY GLICKMAN AT THE MIKE. A young Marty Glickman was on the WHN New York microphone the night of Ernie Calverley's shot. A great Olympic track athlete in 1936, Glickman has a broadcasting career that spanned more than 50 years and included worldwide coverage of all sports. When asked in 1990 about the shot, he wrote, "It is still the most exciting moment in my broadcasting career." This rendering of Glickman was on the cover of the Madison Square Garden program when the Rams visited the following year.

MADISON SQUARE GARDEN

ST. JOHN'S vs. RHODE ISLAND STATE
NEW YORK U. vs. SOUTHERN METHODIST

JANUARY 4, 1947

24¢, N. Y. C. SALES TAX 1¢ **25**¢

AWAITING THE RETURNING HEROES. All who remained in Kingston during Rhody's game against Bowling Green University were glued to their radios. When the final buzzer sounded, the normally tranquil campus erupted. At noon the next day, the student body, faculty, and Kingston villagers descended upon the Kingston station to greet their heroes. This picture shows the cheerleaders revving up the crowd as the train comes into sight. Moments later, a motorcade traveled the two miles up college hill for a huge pep rally on the quadrangle.

ERNIE CALVERLEY'S PATENTED SHOT. This action took place a few nights after Rhode Island's game against Bowling Green, in the NIT semifinal game against Muhlenberg, which was won by the Rams. Ernie Calverley cashed in 27 points. This photograph portrays his patented one-hand runner from above the key. Filling the lane is Dick Hole. (Courtesy Providence Journal.)

RELAXING BEFORE THE NIT FINAL. Rhode Island State's opponent in the 1946 NIT final was one of the nation's top teams, the University of Kentucky Wildcats, coached by the legendary Adolph Rupp. Coach Frank Keaney believed that trips to New York City offered too many distractions. "Don't be looking at tall buildings!" he would rant. He must have been pleased with this card game in the team's hotel. From left to right, are Sal Sclafani, Jackie Allen, Dick Hole, Tommy Baker, Ernie Calverley, Al Nichols, Bob Shea, and Al Palmieri.

ERNIE CALVERLEY IN THE GARDEN SPOTLIGHT. Every player's dream is to be introduced in a big arena before a big game. Here is Ernie Calverley, dribbling to center court, after his introduction to 18,000 New York fans before the 1946 NIT final. A large contingent of Ram fans had traveled on the "Rhody Special" to attend the game. In addition, thousands of New Yorkers had adopted the underdog Keaneymen and cheered for them throughout the game.

CALVERLEY FAST-BREAKS KENTUCKY. In action against Kentucky, Ernie Calverley leads the fast break and dishes a pass to Dick Hole for a layup. Ralph Beard, Kentucky's All-American guard, did a great job of denying Calverley the ball, but the other Rams picked up the action and took the Wildcats to the wire before succumbing 46-45. (Courtesy Providence Journal.)

ERNIE CALVERLEY, MVP. The heartbreak of losing to Kentucky in the NIT championship game was salved when the New York press corps gave Ernie Calverley (left) the Most Valuable Player Award. Coach Frank Keaney admires Calverley's new silver ware. A week later Calverley was named first team All-American and was invited to play in the annual Madison Square Garden College All-Star Game. He went on to play professionally for the Providence Steamrollers of the Basketball Association of America.

MORE HONORS FOR THE RAMS. The Boston Garden held college doubleheaders during the 1940s. In a classic January 1946 duel between New England's two best, Rhode Island defeated Holy Cross 65-58. The Boston Garden chose an All-Garden Team for the season. Both Ernie Calverley and Dick Hole were named, along with the Crusaders' Joe Mullaney. This drawing appeared in the 1946–1947 Boston Garden program.

THE 1945-1946 ALL-GARDEN TEAM

DICK HOLE
RHODE ISLAND STATE
FORWARD

SID TANENBAUM
NEW YORK U.
FORWARD

ERNIE CALVERLY
RHODE ISLAND STATE
CENTER

JOE MULLANEY
HOLY CROSS
GUARD

BOB DILLE
VALPARAISO
GUARD

THE 1946–1947 STARTING FIVE. Ernie Calverley and Bob Shea graduated, but the Rams continued to be one of the top teams in the East, winning 17 games and losing only 3. The starting five, from left to right, are Sal Sclafani, Dick Hole, Ken Goodwin, Jackie Allen, and Al Palmieri. Hole, from Newport, scored 1,152 points in only three seasons of play, and Goodwin rang up 1,170 career points.

ARM IN ARM IN MADISON SQUARE GARDEN. The Rams continued their annual treks to New York's Madison Square Garden, usually to face coach Joe Lapchick and his teams from St. John's. This January 1947 game action shows Rhody's Don Shannon locking arms with Larry Jacobson. Rhode Island won the game 54-50. Don was one of four Shannon brothers from Pawtucket to play for the Rams between 1939 and 1954. The other three were Earl, Bill, and Bob Shannon.

KEANEY'S LAST TEAM, 1947–1948. Coach Frank Keaney (back left) decided to step down in the spring of 1948 after 28 years at the helm of the Rams. His successor was his assistant, Robert "Red" Haire (back right). The team won 17 games and lost 6. The players, from left to right, are as follows: (front row) Sal Sclafani, Walt Bassler, Leon Golembiewski, Ken Goodwin, Bruce Blount, and Hank Zabierik; (middle row) Dick Hole, Lou Kelly, Jackie Allen, Don Shannon, and Bill Shannon; (back row) Bill Benesch, Bob Wilson, Dick Rutherford, Walt Bergman, Vin Santo, and Moe Zarchen.

ACTION VERSUS RUTGERS, FEBRUARY 1948. A two-game road trip in early February 1948 nudged Frank Keaney toward his decision to retire as coach. Following a close loss to Rutgers, Keaney had a seizure and needed medical attention. He came through the scare, but he hung up the whistle at season's end. This Rutgers game action shows Dick Hole (11), who stood at six feet one inch, leaping against six-foot-six-inch Bucky Hatchett, Rutgers' top player.

THE MAINE FREEZE NO. 1. Occasionally an opposing coach tried to foil Frank Keaney's two-points-per-minute pace by slowing down the game and "freezing" the ball on offense, even when behind. In 1948, the University of Maine invaded Rodman Hall and employed such tactics. Keaney considered this an affront to the game's integrity. When Rhode Island grabbed the lead, he directed his team to "sit on the ball," literally. Here is Bruce Blount, on the ball, chatting with teammate Sal Sclafani. In the background, Ken Goodwin and Don Shannon visit with the referee. The Rams won the game 48-32.

THE MAINE FREEZE NO. 2. One month later, at Maine, the Black Bears repeated the deep freeze, even though trailing by 29-17 at halftime. Frank Keaney, in "an emotional tither" (his own words), again directed the Rams to "sit on the ball," but there was more. He distributed newspapers to the bench players. Ken Goodwin drop-kicked an attempted shot. Mike Santoro played "Silent Night" on a harmonica. When the referee gave Santoro a technical, he said, "This is a travesty!" to which Santoro replied, "No it's not, it's a harmonica!" Rhode Island won the game 55-43. It was Keaney's 400th career victory. He won once more—a 108-84 win over Providence College—a game much more to his liking. Manager Mike Majkut, the harmonica owner, smiles in the lower right corner.

A KEANEY COLLAGE. This collage appeared in the program for the dedication of Keaney Gymnasium in November 1953. Frank Keaney continued in his position as director of athletics until his retirement in 1956, completing a remarkable 36-year stay at the University of Rhode Island. His basketball teams set many scoring records with their patented firehorse brand of ball. Keaney became known as the "father of the fast break." His players scored over 100

points 29 times. During his coaching era, Rhode Island State College won 223 games in Rodman Hall while losing only 27. Overall, Keaney won 401 and lost 124. He retired from coaching after 28 years, but the tradition of Rhode Island basketball excellence and excitement was well established.

A Tribute to All of Keaney's Men. This drawing by Frank Lanning of the Providence Journal is a lasting tribute to coach Frank Keaney and every one of his basketball players during his 28 years at the helm of the Rhode Island State Rams.

Three

THE YANKEE CONFERENCE YEARS
1948–1975

THE 1949–1950 RAMS. In the late 1940s, the presidents and athletic directors of the six New England land grant colleges began meetings to consider the formation of a new league for athletic competition, appropriately called the Yankee Conference. Rhode Island's president Dr. Carl R. Woodward and athletic director Frank W. Keaney were leading advocates for this alliance. Joining Rhode Island were the state universities of Maine, New Hampshire, Vermont, Massachusetts, and Connecticut. The Yankee Conference became a reality in 1951. Basketball competition among all six schools was automatically scheduled until the dissolution of the league in 1975. Rhode Island won 155 Yankee Conference games and lost 70, while capturing 4 titles and finishing second 11 times. Shown are the 1949–1950 Rams poised for a challenging regional and national schedule. From left to right are Johnny Mitchell, George Handler, Bruce Blount, Leon Golembiewski, Walt Bassler, and Donnie Shannon. Rhody accomplished an 18-8 record.

RED HAIRE, NEW HEAD COACH. Red Haire (center) was appointed head coach in 1948. A Keaney assistant for two years, he had played for Rhode Island in the 1920s. Here, he meets with his two captains, Leon Golembiewski (left) and Bruce Blount. Golembiewski commanded the backboards. Blount was a great all-around player. While a youth in Kingston, he had been the Rams' mascot and towel boy. He still holds the Rhode Island schoolboy record of 67 points in a game. He scored 1,163 points as a Ram, 40 on the all-time list. An ROTC graduate, Blount had an honored career in the U.S. Army, attaining the rank of lieutenant general.

CAPTAIN-ELECT JOHNNY MITCHELL. Johnny Mitchell (center) hailed from Waterville, Maine, where he was an All-State schoolboy star in three sports. Only five feet eight inches tall, he had a tremendous heart and was a natural leader. He is considered one of Rhody's greatest defenders and was always matched with the opponent's best scorer. Here he receives congratulations from outgoing captains Bruce Blount (left) and Leon Golembiewski as he accepts the captaincy of the Rams for the 1950–1951 season.

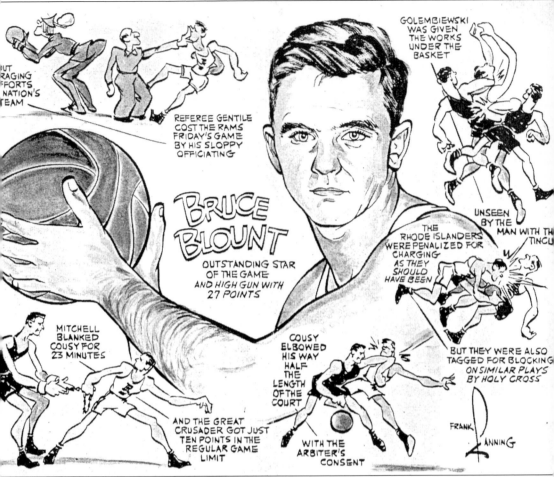

OUT RAGING FORTS NATION'S TEAM

REFEREE GENTILE COST THE RAMS FRIDAY'S GAME BY HIS SLOPPY OFFICIATING

GOLEMBIEWSKI WAS GIVEN THE WORKS UNDER THE BASKET

BRUCE BLOUNT

OUTSTANDING STAR OF THE GAME AND HIGH GUN WITH 27 POINTS

THE RHODE ISLANDERS WERE PENALIZED FOR CHARGING AS THEY SHOULD HAVE BEEN

UNSEEN BY THE MAN WITH THE TINCL

MITCHELL BLANKED COUSY FOR 23 MINUTES

COUSY ELBOWED HIS WAY HALF THE LENGTH OF THE COURT

BUT THEY WERE ALSO TAGGED FOR BLOCKING ON SIMILAR PLAYS BY HOLY CROSS

AND THE GREAT CRUSADER GOT JUST TEN POINTS IN THE REGULAR GAME LIMIT

WITH THE ARBITER'S CONSENT

FRANK LANNING

A CLASSIC GAME AGAINST NO. 1, HOLY CROSS. This Frank Lanning cartoon appeared in the *Providence Journal* on February 18, 1950, following a thrilling game against the nation's top team, Holy Cross. The Crusaders were led by All-American Bob Cousy, one of the greatest collegiate and professional players of all time. Cousy was later inducted into the Naismith Memorial Hall of Fame. Bruce Blount, who scored 27 points, forced the game into overtime with two nothing-but-net free throws at the wire. Johnny Mitchell played one of the greatest defensive games in Rhode Island history, holding Cousy to one field goal in regulation. He fouled out in overtime, and Cousy scored at will to give Holy Cross the victory 70-62. The game was played at the old Rhode Island Auditorium on North Main Street in Providence before a capacity crowd of 6,000.

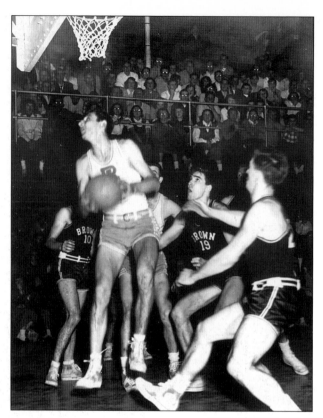

FREDDY CONGLETON REBOUNDING AGAINST BROWN UNIVERSITY. Red Haire stepped down as head coach in 1952 and was replaced by Jack Guy from Bucknell University. Guy inherited two seniors who were well on their way to illustrious Rhody careers: Fred Congleton and Bill Baird. A wiry six-foot-five-inch low-post player, Congleton (with the ball) is pictured during a 90-70 victory over Brown. He accumulated 1,334 career points, currently 30th on the all-time list.

CAPTAIN BILL BAIRD, 1952–1953. Bill Baird, a solid six-footer from Pawtucket, was an offensive machine, standing 18th on the all-time list, with 1,534 points. He eventually returned to his alma mater as freshman coach and assistant to Ernie Calverley. He then moved on to a very successful coaching career at Rhode Island College, where he also served as athletic director.

A POSTSEASON BANQUET FOR THE 1952–1953 RAMS. Jack Guy's first team was the last to play in Rodman Hall. This postseason banquet photograph shows several significant Rhode Island basketball boosters and associates. Shown, from left to right, are the following: (front row) Bill Baird (co-captain), Hugo Manielli (Class of 1930, longtime booster, trustee, and Athletic Council president), Dr. A.A. "Savy" Savastano (Class of 1928, orthopedic surgeon of international reputation who gave a lifetime of medical attention to injured Rhode Island athletes), Frank Keaney (athletic director), Jack Guy (head coach), and Fred Congleton (co-captain); (middle row) Dick Cole (longtime trainer for Ram athletes), Johnny Chapman (athletic department representative), Dave Stenhouse and Ray Rossi and Bernie "Slick" Pina (all team members), Chet Berry (Memorial Student Union director), and Paul Cieurzo (longtime assistant coach); (back row) Danny Dunn, Ed Leiblach, Rollie Kubisky, Art Hellwig, Bill Marine, and Ken Delner (all team members). The team finished second in the Yankee Conference with a 13-10 record.

THE NEW GYMNASIUM NEARS COMPLETION. As Rhode Island basketball entered its second half century, a new home for the Rams was much needed. There was unanimous agreement that the edifice be named for Frank W. Keaney (second from left), who had coached the Rams for 28 years and led them to national prominence. Here, the last piece of steel is about to be lifted into place.

DEDICATION NIGHT FOR KEANEY GYM. Opening night for Frank W. Keaney Gymnasium, December 1, 1953, was a festive affair and included a basketball double-header, with the Rams' three major rivals as the visitors: Providence College, Brown University, and the University of Connecticut (URI's foe). Coincidentally, the last three games played in Rodman Hall the previous winter had been against these three teams—all Rhody wins. Dr. Harold Browning (right foreground), university vice-president, presents a plaque to Frank Keaney while Dr. Carl Woodward (background, between the two), university president, looks on.

THE KEANEY GYM DEDICATION PROGRAM. Frank Lanning, Providence Journal cartoonist and great friend of URI sports, offered this wonderful rendering of the new gym, with the Menty looking down with humble pride on this monument to his greatness as a teacher and coach.

A FINAL LESSON FROM THE MENTY. Shortly before his 1956 retirement as athletic director, Frank Keaney (center) offers some advice to two Rams players in Keaney Gym. Dave Stenhouse (left) from Westerly, was a solid guard and also an excellent baseball player, who headed for a career as a major league pitcher. Eric Anderson was a forward from New York City. Keaney's full tenure at URI was 36 years, from 1920 to 1956.

47

A ONE-TWO PUNCH FROM JERSEY. The 1954–1955 Rams' starting five, from left to right, are Ron Marozzi, Eric Anderson, Dave Stenhouse, Billy Von Weyhe, and Bobby Serra. Von Weyhe, a "smooth as silk" forward from New Jersey, poured in 1,656 points for the Rams from 1954 to 1957. He is 13th on the all-time career scoring list and the all-time URI leader in points per game (22.6). His classmate Marozzi, also from New Jersey, scored 1,639 career points and is 14th on the all-time list.

TOM HARRINGTON, RECORD BREAKER. On February 11, 1959, Tom Harrington rewrote the record book with a thrilling 50-point performance as the Rams defeated Brandeis University 119-106. He broke the all-time single game record of 48 points set in 1943 by Ernie Calverley, his head coach, who had a court side seat as his record fell. Somewhat overshadowed was the 35 points scored by Barry Multer. Harrington's name appears 12 times in the Rhody record book. He is 10th in all-time scoring averages, at 21.9 points per game.

PRESIDENT HORN'S ALMA MATER COMES TO KINGSTON. University of Rhode Island president Francis Horn (center) poses for the honorary center jump. A rabid sports fan and devoted alumnus of Dartmouth College, he arranged for the Rams to play his alma mater on December 19, 1959. Pictured with him, from left to right, are Rhode Island center Gary Koenig, Dartmouth's legendary coach Alvin "Doggie" Julian, Rhode Island coach Ernie Calverley, and the unidentified Dartmouth center.

NCAA TIME IN MADISON SQUARE GARDEN, MARCH 1961. The 1960–1961 Rams beat the University of Connecticut in the last regular season game and captured the college's first Yankee Conference title with a 9-1 mark, qualifying for their first-ever NCAA berth. They played a powerful St. Bonaventure team in Madison Square Garden. This photograph shows Rhody's Dave Ricereto going high to score on a driving layup. The Rams kept the game close throughout but eventually fell to the Bonnies 86-76.

49

URI'S FIRST NCAA TEAM. Coach Ernie Calverley's 1960–1961 Rams won 18 and lost 9, becoming the first URI NCAA tournament team. The team is pictured, from left to right, as follows: (front row) Mike Weiss, Dave Ricereto, Barry Multer (captain), Gary Koenig, and Charlie Lee; (back row) Ernie Calverley (coach), Stu Schachter, Nat Smith, Bob Logan, Ron Stenhouse, Bill Nicynski, Tony Lasale, and Bill Baird (assistant coach). The team's makeup was formidable, including three all-time scoring leaders and an all-time rebound leader. Ricereto scored 1,535 career points, 17th on the list. Charlie Lee poured in 1,453, 21st of all-time. Barry Multer rang up 1,352 points, 27th on the career list. Gary Koenig is second on the all-time rebounding list, with 1,039. He holds the record for rebounds per game at 13.3.

A New Scoreboard for Keaney Gym. Coach Ernie Calverley (left) and Morris Zarchen (right), athletic director, admire the new scoreboard about to be hoisted to the rafters over center court in 1962. Both men played for the Rams in the 1940s. Calverley's coaching stint for his alma mater covered 11 seasons, from 1957 to 1968, and resulted in 154 wins against 125 losses. He stands second behind his mentor, Frank Keaney, in all-time Rhode Island victories.

Traveling with Class. Looking good on and off the court was Ernie Calverley's way. Dressed in their Ram blue blazers and Rhode Island ties, Ernie Calverley (right), sports information director Tom Doherty (left) and the 1963–1964 Rams pose for a photograph before departing for a road game.

STEVE CHUBIN. Steve Chubin (left) played for Ernie Calverley during the mid-1960s. Later, he became Rhode Island's all-time career scoring leader, a position he holds to this day. A strong operative around the basket, as well as a scorer with good range, Chubin poured in 2,154 points in just three seasons. Pictured in 1964 with Calverley, Chubin holds the Look Magazine Award he earned for his second straight year as an All-East selection.

UNIVERSITY OF CONNECTICUT PLAYOFF TICKETS IN HOT DEMAND. The rivalry between URI and the University of Connecticut has been one of the greatest in New England basketball history. The two teams have played 144 times, with Rhode Island winning 65 and UConn 79. No games were more bitterly contested than the three played during the 1963–1964 season. UConn won at home 43-41. Rhode Island won at home in the last game of the regular season 54-53, gaining a tie for the Yankee Conference title. The playoff game for the NCAA bid was held four days later in Keaney Gym. Shown are Rhody fans waiting in line for the cherished ducats.

URI versus **UConn, March 1964.** In Keaney Gym a standing-room-only crowd looks on as the Rams and the Huskies vie for the cherished NCAA bid in March 1964. Rhody's Steve Chubin (right) floats a perfect pass to a posted up Larry Johnson during the waning minutes. The Huskies had a good run down the stretch and broke the hearts of Ram fans with a 61-60 victory. Rhody got its revenge two years later under similar circumstances.

THE 1964–1965 STARTING FIVE. The 1964–1965 starting five, from left to right, are Dennis McGovern, John Mulfinger, Frank Nightingale, Jimmy Cymbala, and Mike Fitzgerald. Coach Ernie Calverley enjoyed eight straight winning seasons, including 1964–1965, in spite of the loss of Steve Chubin for the season. Dennis McGovern, a prolific scorer from Coventry, Rhode Island, compiled a career total of 1,696 points, 12th all-time. Mike Fitzgerald scored 1,191 points, 38th on the career list. Jimmy Cymbala was a fine point guard and an exceptional free throw shooter, second in all-time percentage at .820.

ANOTHER UCONN PLAYOFF GAME. In 1966, it was yet again a familiar March Madness scenario: the Connecticut Huskies and the Rhode Island Rams locked in a classic struggle for a coveted NCAA bid. Tied with their nutmeg neighbors for first in the Yankee Conference, the Rams traveled to Storrs for the decisive game. This was Rhody's turn to meet the challenge. Led by Steve Chubin, seen here scoring on a put-back rebound, the Rams won 67-62.

A DOSE OF CHUBIN FOR HUSKIE FANS. Steve Chubin scores from the foul line in the March 1966 playoff game before a packed house in the Connecticut Fieldhouse, a venue that had been none too friendly to Rhode Island. Just three days before, the Rams had lost on the same floor 96-74, a game that forced the playoff. In fact, this was the Rams' first win in Storrs since 1958.

A JOYFUL WELCOME BACK IN KINGSTON. A huge midnight celebration awaited the Rams as their bus pulled up to Keaney Gym following their March 1966 game at the University of Connecticut, a victory that clinched their bid to the NCAA Tournament. The game ball and the nets from the Connecticut Fieldhouse evoked a thunderous cheer from the Rhody faithful.

ART STEPHENSON, REBOUNDER EXTRAORDINAIRE. Art Stephenson, an all-time Rhody great, wore the Keaney blue from 1965 to 1968. Although only six feet five inches tall, he played a game well above his height. The greatest rebounder in the Rams' storied history, Stephenson holds the following records: most rebounds in game (28), most in a season (420), and most in a career (1,048). In addition, he is eighth on the all-time scoring list, with 1,776 points. It is said that he invented the "double-double" at URI, consistently scoring and rebounding in double figures.

THE 1965–1966 RAMS. Coach Ernie Calverley completed his coaching career in 1968 with his eighth straight winning season and a first-place finish in the Yankee Conference. The 1965–1966 NCAA-bound Rams, from left to right, are as follows: (front row) co-captains Mike Fitzpatrick and Jimmy Cymbala; (middle row) trainer Dick Cole, coach Ernie Calverley, Henry Carey, Ted Haglund, Richy Cranit, Robert Boehn, Steve Chubin, assistant coach Vincent Cazetta, and manager Russell Haber; (back row) Larry Johnson, Donnie Kaull, Tom Khroner, Bob Knight, Art Stephenson, Steve Kropitko, Leslie McPhee, and Ron Oliver.

NEW RAM COACH TOM CARMODY. Ernie Calverley retired as head coach at the end of the 1968 season, and the university hired Tom Carmody (center), an assistant at Duke University, to take over the Rhode Island program. Here he is greeted by players Joe Zaranka (left) and Claude English. Carmody coached the Rams for five seasons. English became a co-captain two years later.

YANKEE CONFERENCE ACTION, 1970. The Rams and the Huskies, perennial leaders in the Yankee Conference, were challenged in the late 1960s and early 1970s by the University of Massachusetts. The Minutemen were led by Julius "Dr. J." Irving, destined to become one of basketball's all-time greats, and Al Skinner, a future ABA and NBA player, who was destined to become URI's head coach. In this Keaney Gym action, Dwight Tollman (12) glides in for a lay-up with Nate Adger (32) and John Fultz (30) following up.

1969–1970 Co-Captains Claude English and John Fultz. The two Ram leaders, Claude English (left) and John Fultz, pose outside Keaney Gym. English, blessed with a tremendous jumping ability, later served as a URI assistant coach and head coach in 1981. Fultz, a prolific scorer from all over the floor, stands sixth on the all-time points list, with 1,834, and second in points per game average at 22.4. His most remarkable performance was against the UConn Huskies on March 1, 1969, when he netted 46 points in a 92-72 romp.

Holy Cross Crusaders Invade Kingston. The history of Rhode Island basketball has included many exciting contests with Holy Cross. From 1946 to 1949, the Rams received an annual invitation to play the Crusaders in the Boston Garden. Several games were played in Kingston. This action took place during the 1970 contest in Keaney Gym, a game the Rams won in thrilling style, 88-87. Bill Bird (33) goes high to swat away an attempted layup.

THE KEANEY "KRAZIES." For most of Keaney Gym's illustrious basketball history, the students had the best seats in the house—right on top of the action at courtside, wedged in on pullout bleachers. This picture captures the excitement and zaniness of it all. During time-outs, opposing coaches had their players drag chairs to the foul circle to improve their chances of being heard.

1971–1972 TRI-CAPTAINS. Coach Tom Carmody (foreground) poses with his three captains, from left to right, Phil Hickson, Steve Rowell, and Abu Bakr, before the start of the 1971–1972 season. A Yankee Conference crown lay ahead. Hickson was a great shooter who managed 1,335 career points, 29th on URI's all-time list. Rowell was a great pressure player and uncanny shooter. Bakr, a solid inside player and rebounder, has served his alma mater as a counselor and administrator. He remains close to the basketball program and frequently serves as television color analyst for Ram games.

ROWELL DRIVES ON TEMPLE. This 1973 action shot shows Steve Rowell, with his patented drive to the hoop, against Temple University before a packed Keaney Gym. Following the play are Robbie Young and Abu Bakr. Temple prevailed 93-80. Rowell, one of Rhody's most brilliant players, scored a career 1,890 points, fourth on the all-time list.

JIM NORMAN, "VOICE OF THE RAMS." As an undergraduate Jim Norman, Class of 1957, broadcast four years of Ram football and basketball games on the student radio station. Hired soon after his graduation as a sports information assistant, Norman took over the Ram sports microphone, announcing 1,286 games over 34 years until his retirement in 1995. He served as sports information director for 22 years.

CHUBIN, ROWELL, AND CALVERLEY. Frank Lanning rendered this drawing in 1979 of the Rams' three all-time scoring leaders at that time. Steve Chubin, who played in the 1960s, scored 2,154 points and remains the all-time scoring leader to this day. Steve Rowell tallied 1,890 points during his career in the early 1970s and is currently fourth on the all-time list. The legendary Ernie Calverley amassed his total of 1,868 points during the 1940s and stands fifth all-time. Calverley had a good view of Chubin's exploits as his coach.

A Ram Fan's Delight: Keaney Gym, a Packed House, a Providence College Game.
The Friars and the Rams played home-and-home games in virtually every season from
1934–1935 to 1979–1980. Thereafter, new league alignments for both teams resulted in
scheduling difficulties and there has been a single annual contest since. All games were played
in the respective campus gyms until the 1974–1975 season, when the new Providence Civic
Center became the venue, allowing for larger crowds to enjoy the intense rivalry. Shown is the
February 1962 game at Keaney Gym, played before a record 5,000 fans and won by Rhode
Island 71-61.

Four

THE KRAFT YEARS
1973–1981

A NEW DIRECTION, A NEW COACH. The mid 1970s marked a time of league realignment for Rhode Island basketball. The Yankee Conference was about to dissolve, and the university leaders were interested in upgrading the overall level of competition. The Eastern Collegiate Athletic Conference (ECAC) became the answer. Key rivals were St. John's, Boston College, Holy Cross, and the University of Connecticut. By the late 1970s, the Eastern Eight Conference was formed. Along with the University of Rhode Island, the new league included the University of Pittsburgh, Rutgers University, West Virginia, Duquesne, St. Bonaventure, George Washington, and the University of Massachusetts. Jack Kraft had been lured from Villanova to succeed Tom Carmody as head coach. He led the Rams for nine seasons until 1982. In this photograph he instructs his charges during a time-out.

SOARING AGAINST BROWN UNIVERSITY, 1976. In spite of considerable schedule reshuffling in the mid-1970s, Rhode Island continued its traditional rivalries with Brown University, Providence College, and the University of Connecticut. Here Vic Soares (21) goes up for a jumper against the Bruins in the opening game of the 1976–1977 season. The Rams beat Brown 78-74.

GOODBYE TO YANKEE CONFERENCE TEAMS. The 1975–1976 season marked the last visit to Keaney Gym by several teams in the Yankee Conference. In this game against the Maine Black Bears, won by Rhode Island 79-69, Rhody's Stan Wright attacks the basket, as Carlton Smith (32) and Jim "Jiggy" Williamson (23) follow the play.

STAN WRIGHT, IMPACT PLAYER. In this January 1976 drawing, *Providence Journal* cartoonist Frank Lanning highlights Wright's prowess and versatility as a rebounder, assist leader, and scorer. Only a sophomore at the time, Wright helped lead the Rams back to national prominence throughout his career. He netted 1,346 points, 28th on the all-time list.

RAMS TANGLE WITH ST. JOHN'S, 1976. By the mid-1970s, most "big games" at home were scheduled for the Providence Civic Center. Here, Jiggy Williamson (23) goes up for a shot against St. John's. The rivalry, big in the 1940s, had been renewed with home-and-home exchanges several years before. The January 31, 1974, game, played in Keaney Gym, ended on February 1—the only collegiate game to be completed the morning after a rain delay. The gym's roof could not handle the nor'easter that blew in, literally, during the game. St. John's won the game 77-59.

THE RAMETTES SWING INTO ACTION. In the 1970s, the Ramettes were formed to add to the spirit and color of basketball games. These Rhody gals featured chorus line dancing to lively music. The Ramettes still entertain Ram fans with their energetic and acrobatic routines.

URI-PC Hoops. The annual clash between the Rams and the Providence College Friars has traditionally been the top sports event in the state. Bragging rights are at stake for each college's alumni, many of whom work side by side in government, business, and the service industry. In fact, most Rhode Islanders take sides, and the intensity of the rivalry can be felt for several days leading up to tipoff time. Shown is a packed Providence Civic Center (12,150 capacity) as the two adversaries battle in the mid-1970s. Between 1974 and 1980, when two games a year were played at the Civic Center (plus one playoff game), the Rams won six and the Friars seven.

RETIRING NO. 3. Only one URI men's basketball jersey has been retired: Ernie Calverley's famous No. 3. Ernie Calverley (left) played for Rams from 1942 to 1946. He set a national scoring record, was a two-time All-American, and hit his famous 62-foot shot at the buzzer in the 1946 NIT, still known as "the shot heard 'round the world." He is the second winningest URI coach and is still introduced as Mr. URI Basketball. With him are his wife, Jean Calverley, and longtime Ram announcer Jim Norman, doing the honors.

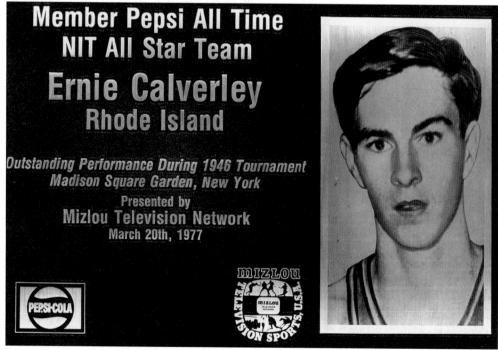

Member Pepsi All Time
NIT All Star Team
Ernie Calverley
Rhode Island

Outstanding Performance During 1946 Tournament
Madison Square Garden, New York
Presented by
Mizlou Television Network
March 20th, 1977

AN ALL-TIME NIT ALL-STAR. This plaque was presented to Ernie Calverley in 1977 at a special Madison Square Garden reunion of players who achieved the greatest performances at National Invitational Tournaments. Until the early 1950s, the NIT was considered the top prestige tournament for college teams. In the early years, when Rhode Island played in four NITs, only eight elite teams from across the country were invited.

BALL BOYS AND BALL GIRLS, 1979. Involving the community's youth in the basketball program has been a Rhode Island tradition. Future Rhody students help distribute the balls for pregame and halftime shooting practice, and towel down the floor when there are slippery spots. Each summer, the Rams conduct weekly camps for boys and girls of all ages.

A SOLID CORE FOR COACH KRAFT. The 1976–1977 Rams were led by tri-captains Jiggy Williamson (23), Lem Johnson (33), and Stan Wright (24). With this talented threesome, coach Jack Kraft built a program that became one of Rhode Island's finest. After a 13-13 season, the Rams won 24 games the following year and achieved their first NCAA bid since 1966.

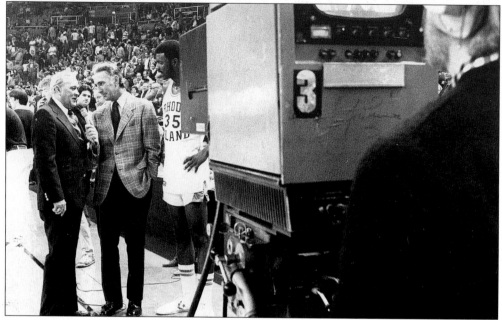

"SLY" JOINS THE RAMS. In 1976, Sylvester "Sly" Williams from New Haven, Connecticut, was a highly sought recruit. Providence College had high hopes of signing him. Williams had other thoughts and decided to stop in Kingston and become a Rhode Island Ram. He proved to be one of Rhody's all-time greats. This unusual photograph shows a television interview following a Rhode Island game. Coach Jack Kraft (left) and Williams (35) are being interviewed by hall-of-famer Bob Cousy.

FURIOUS ACTION VERSUS THE FRIARS, 1977. Jim "Jiggy" Williamson (23) was listed at five feet eleven inches but played above his height. He was a scoring point guard who could hit from anywhere on the floor. Fans recall his amazing shots under pressure. He scored 1,531 career points, 19th on the all-time list. Here, he skies and dishes a pass to Noel Taylor (30).

ECAC ACTION VERSUS FAIRFIELD UNIVERSITY, 1978. An automatic NCAA bid awaited the winner of the New England Eastern Collegiate Athletic Conference (ECAC) tournament. Rhody played Fairfield University on March 2, and prevailed 71-69. This action shows Sly Williams taking the ball to the hoop. The victory moved Rhody to the final, played two nights later against the Providence College Friars.

SLY WILLIAMS REBOUNDS IN THE CHAMPIONSHIP GAME. In this critical ECAC playoff game against Providence College on March 4, 1978, Sly Williams (35) demonstrates his power under the boards as he leads the Rams to a thrilling 65-62 victory to capture the New England championship and earn an automatic bid to the NCAA Tournament.

CUTTING DOWN THE NETS AND EMBARRASSING THE RHODE ISLAND SENATE. The 1978 Rhody play-off victory over the intrastate rival Friars, which earned the automatic NCAA bid, was certainly sweet. Equally sweet was the embarrassment the Rams caused the Rhode Island State Senate, which had issued a resolution wishing Providence College much success and prosperity, but not one word for the state university. A gleeful Rhody fan holds the sign that says, "R.I. Senate, you lost 12,000 votes. URI #1."

TO THE VICTORS GO THE AWARDS. There is joy in the hearts of Rhody players and their adoring fans as newly won hardware is hoisted following the Rams' stunning win over Providence College on March 4, 1978. A few days later, the NCAA draw assigned them a formidable opponent, Duke University, with the first-round game to be played in Charlotte, North Carolina. Celebrating, from left to right, are Phil Kydd, Jimmy Wright, Perry Davis, and Randy Wilds.

SYLVESTER "SLY" WILLIAMS, MVP. There were smiles all around for Sly Williams as he was named the Most Valuable Player in the Eastern Collegiate Athletic Conference playoff in March 1978. Over the season, Williams had scored 564 points and grabbed 255 rebounds to lead his team into the NCAA Championship Tournament. Among other honors, he also garnered the Converse All-American and Player of the Year, New England.

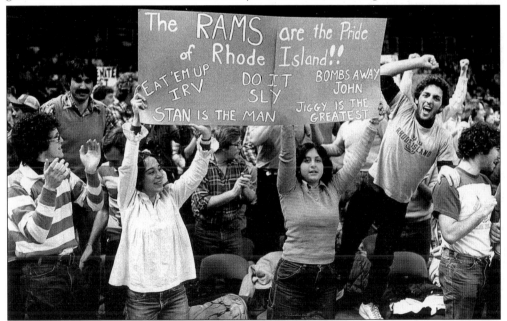

RAM PRIDE RULES, MARCH 1978. Basketball had always been the centerpiece of campus life in Kingston, and Ram pride hit a fever pitch as coach Jack Kraft prepared his charges for the trek to Charlotte, North Carolina, for a first-round game against Duke University. The sign implores Irv (Chatman), Stan (Wright), Sly (Williams), John (Nelson), and Jiggy (Williamson) to get after the Blue Devils.

SLY WILLIAMS MEETS THE BLUE DEVILS. It was madness in March as the Rams tangled with powerful Duke University in the first round of the 1978 NCAA Championships. Sly Williams had lived up to his billing as a superb basketball player, and he was not about to disappoint a national television audience. He always played with a powerful presence and an elegant style. Witness this classic form as he launches a jump shot in heavy traffic against Duke. Eugene Banks vainly tries to block the shot, while super center Mike Gminski (43) and Bob Bender (21) of Duke, and Williams's teammates Percy Davis (left) and Stan Wright (24) look on. The Rams took highly ranked and heavily favored Duke to the wire, losing a heartbreaker 63-62. Duke was the eventual tournament runner-up. Williams ended his Rhody career the following season. A two-time All-American, he totaled 1,777 points, seventh best of all-time. In the 1978–1979 season, he scored 693 points, third on the all-time list, averaging 23.9, the second highest in Rhody hoop history.

THE 1978–1979 RAMS BOUND FOR THE POSTSEASON. The following season Rhode Island continued to play on a national stage. Tackling arguably their strongest schedule ever, they posted a 20-9 record and advanced to the second round of the ECAC Championship Tournament. There, they lost a rubber match to traditional rival UConn, a game which denied them a return to the NCAA. They did get an NIT bid, and were pitted against the University of Maryland at the Terrapins' Cole Fieldhouse. The game was a white knuckler, extending into three overtimes before the Rams succumbed 67-65. Shown is the team, from left to right, as follows: (front row) Bill Hahn (assistant coach), Claude English (associate coach), Irv Chatman and John Nelson and Sly Williams (all tri-captains), and Jack Kraft (head coach); (middle row) Mike Rule (trainer), Nicky Johnson, Kevin Whiting, Willie Middlebrooks, Ed Bednarcik, Vic Bertuglio, and John Cazetta and Bill Rickley (both team managers); (back row) Lanauze Hollis, Derek Groomes, Jimmy Wright, Roland Houston, Gilson DeJesus, and Phil Kydd.

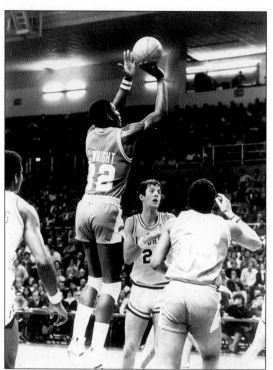

JIMMY WRIGHT SHOOTS AT EXPLORERS. Rhode Island's Jimmy Wright, who starred at forward for the Rams from 1977–1981, goes up for a jumper against LaSalle University in this 1979 game, as Phil Kydd (15) prepares to rebound. The Rams won a thriller 83-80. Wright had a distinguished career, scoring 1,333 points, 32nd on the all-time list. He also was a great rebounder, picking off 773 caroms, the fifth all-time best for the Rams.

THE END OF A SPECIAL RIVALRY. This January 1981 game against UConn ended a streak of 66 straight years, dating back to the 1915–1916 season, in which the Rams and the Huskies had battled on the hardwoods. Over that time they played a total of 139 games, the Rams winning 65 and losing 74. Here, Horace "Pappy" Owens (21) passes to Gilson DeJesus. Owens, a great point guard for the Rams from 1979 to 1983, is ninth on the career scoring list, with 1,765 points.

THE 1980–1981 RAMS, NIT BOUND. The transitions in college basketball league alignments found Rhode Island a member of the Eastern Eight in the winter of 1980–1981. Coach Jack Kraft, starting his eighth season at the helm, coached his final game—sadly, the first contest of the season. Heart problems sidelined him for the rest of the year, and associate coach Claude English, a star for Rhode Island in the late 1960s, was named interim coach and led the team to a 21-win season and the college's seventh NIT bid. It was "one and out" for the Rams at Purdue. Kraft resigned at season's end, and English was elevated to head coach. A tradition of Rhode Island teams posing midst the natural beauty of the Ocean State had begun. Pictured on the rocks at Narragansett are Gilson DeJesus, Wendall Walters, Pete Torncello, Horace "Pappy" Owens, Jimmy Wright, Kevin Compton, Steve Nisbet, Chris Cummings, Phil Kydd, Chris Metcalf, Jack Kraft (head coach), John Monk, Marc Upshaw, Fran Fraschilla (assistant coach), Kevin Whiting, Roland Houston, Claude English (associate coach).

UPSHAW GOES UP AGAINST THE ORANGEMEN. In this January 1980 game against Syracuse University, Mark Upshaw, a premier Rhody guard during the early 1980s, lifts for a jumper at the Providence Civic Center. The Orangemen prevailed 64-54. Upshaw scored 1,363 career points, 26th on the all-time Rhody list.

THE RAMS CAPTURE THE GOVERNOR'S CUP. Following the 1979–1980 season, Rhode Island and Providence College ended their home-and-home format. For their annual contest, a new prize was established: a Governor's Cup. In January 1981, the Rams defeated the Friars in an overtime thriller 53-44. Here, they celebrate, flanked by URI's president Frank Newman (left), and Providence College's president Thomas Peterson. Others enjoying the moment, from left to right, are Irv Chatman (44), Jimmy Wright (32), Phil Kydd, and interim coach Claude English.

Five

WOMEN'S BASKETBALL

ARRIVES

THE FIRST UNDEFEATED TEAM, 1937. Members of the 1937 undefeated women's team, from left to right, are as follows: (front row) Elinor Williams, Janet Potter, Elizabeth Cowell, Gertrude Cooper, Grace O'Connor, Claire Wordell, Ruth Jerrett, and Elsie Brindle; (back row) Geraldine Foley, Marjorie Dunn, Ariadne Panteleiff, Winifred Gregson, Rosalind Waters, Dorothy Keyes, Anna Emma, and Bessie Taylor (manager). Rhody won all 11 games that season. The first evidence of basketball on campus, in 1902, was a "girls' team," two years prior to a "boys' team." By 1920, men's basketball had achieved varsity status and women's basketball had evolved toward intramural and interclass formats, with all-star teams chosen toward winter's end to play a few collegiate rivals. By 1930, the women were playing varsity intercollegiate schedules, and they capped their with undefeated seasons in 1937 and 1939. Following World War II, the women's programs focused on "play days," weekend events in which several collegiate teams played a series of round-robin games. In the mid-1970s, the enactment by Congress of Title IX of the Civil Rights Act assured gender equity in extracurricular activities at all public institutions. For the first time, Rhode Island women's basketball offered full scholarships to its student-athletes.

COACH'S CHALK TALK, 1954. Throughout basketball's early decades, women's rules differed from men's. Women started six players—three on offense and three on defense. The center court line was literally the dividing line between the two. The ball had to be advanced across the line from the defense to the offense. Defensive players therefore never shot the ball. When Title IX gave women's basketball equal status in 1974, women's rules became similar to men's, greatly enhancing the pace of the game.

PRACTICING FOR PLAY DAY. This 1961 photograph shows Rhode Island coeds practicing their shooting in Rodman Gymnasium in preparation for a play day. When the men's team moved to Keaney Gym in 1953, the women's physical education program moved from Lippitt Hall to Rodman Hall. Eventually, the women's athletics were headquartered at the Keaney and Tootell complex.

RHODE ISLAND STATE VERSUS PEMBROKE. This 1946 game against Pembroke College illustrates the six-person lineup—three on offense and three on defense. The game was played in Lippitt Hall, the original campus gym.

THE INAUGURAL SEASON UNDER TITLE IX, 1975–1976. The Rams had fine success in their first varsity season, achieving a 13-8 record against mostly New England opponents. Coach Beth Bricker (center) gives instructions to her team during the Bridgewater State game, won by Rhode Island 104-46, a 58-point margin. Later in the season, Rhody reached the century mark again, beating Maine 103-65, again by 58 points. This same margin of victory was achieved a third time in a win over St. Bonaventure (120-62) in March 1994.

LINDA LOUISE ROWELL, A RHODY STANDOUT. Linda Rowell completed her playing days at URI in 1976 as Rhody's all-time scoring leader. An outstanding shooter and rebounder, she was referred to as "all everything" in her junior year, as her team compiled an 18-2 record. As captain her senior year, she averaged 20.1 points and 19 rebounds per game. She was selected as one of the top 20 players in the East and was invited to the U.S. Olympic basketball trials. She is pictured with her husband, Steve Rowell, who starred for the men's team in the early 1970s, in Rockport, Massachusetts, where they both attended high school. (Photograph by Nora Lewis.)

RHODY'S 1976–1977 TEAM. Rhody pride shows in the faces of these trailblazers for URI women's basketball. Pictured, from left to right, are (front row) Phyllis Douglas, Laurie Cason, unidentified, Lauren Pelchat, Sue Field, and Nancy Caklos; (back row) Kathleen Walling (assistant coach), Michelina Gargiulo, Kim Nelson, Maryanne Kluge, Barbara Walton, unidentified, and Beth Bricker (coach). The Rams won 13 and lost 11.

COACH LANGHAM, RHODY'S NEW COACH. Coach Nancy Langham (second from right), who coached the Rams from 1977 to 1985, is the winningest all-time coach for URI, accumulating 122 wins against 105 losses. Particularly noteworthy is her teams' 9 and 2 record against the Connecticut Huskies. She came to Kingston after a successful stint as head coach at Cortland State in upstate New York.

ACTION AT THE PROVIDENCE CIVIC CENTER. In the early years, women's basketball struggled in its efforts to attract publicity and a following, but ultimately the aesthetically pleasing playing style and the contagious enthusiasm with which the women played appealed to basketball aficionados and attracted loyal supporters. A genuine community spirit began to embrace the players and the coaches.

THE 1979–1980 TEAM LEADERS. Tri-Captains Kim Nelson (12), Kimberly Dick (43), and Elizabeth Phelps (35) pose with head coach Nancy Langham. Dick scored 1,009 career points, accomplished in three seasons, and is 12th on the all-time list. She is also 10th in field goals scored and eighth in field goal percentage (.450).

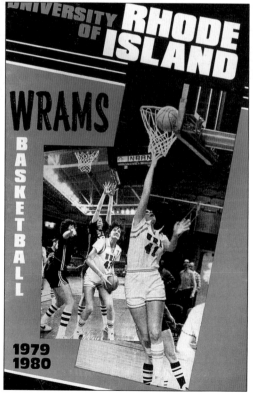

MEDIA GUIDE FOR THE 1979–1980 WRAMS. Basketball media guides were important publications for the promotion of the women's program. This is the cover of one of the earliest issues. As intercollegiate women's hoops took giant growing steps in the 1980s, recruiting became very competitive. Media guides were useful in convincing young women of the attractiveness of playing at the University of Rhode Island. The team used the moniker "WRams" for several seasons to signify the women Rams. The contradiction of the two words led to its demise.

84

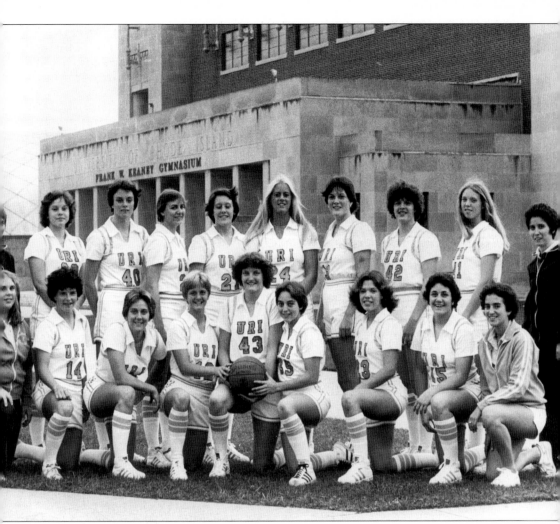

THE 1979–1980 UNIVERSITY OF RHODE ISLAND RAMS. Members of the 1979–1980 team, from left to right, are as follows: (front row) Lisa Rohatsch (team manager), Heather Mahan, Dawn Clark, Kim Nelson, Kim Dick, Beth Phelps, Elyse Dowd, Chris Dinoto, and Chris DiComes (student trainer); (back row) Nancy Langham (coach), Terri Calvert, Naomi Graves, Terri Hutchinson, Lee Gallagher, Mary Beehan, Kathy Mahoney, Joan Ziehl, Debbie Arpert, and Maryanne Cunningham (assistant coach). Missing from the photograph is Maureen Sullivan. The team was well traveled, participating in invitational tournaments at Montclair State (New Jersey), Wyoming, Syracuse, and Vermont. In all, 17 games were played on the road. A successful season was accomplished with a 16 and 11 record.

THE 1981–1982 RAM COACHING STAFF.
Assistant coaches Bob Schneck and Maryanne
Cunningham (center) join head coach Nancy
Langham as they prepare for the 1981–1982
season. Cunningham and Langham were
entering their fifth season at Rhode Island, while
Schneck was starting his first year as an assistant
in basketball and as head coach of women's
volleyball. Eventually, he focused solely on
volleyball, a sport in which he has had a long
run of success.

**NAOMI GRAVES, WRAM ALL-TIME
GREAT.** A four-year star from 1978–1982,
Naomi Graves set a host of basketball
records. She heads the all-time list for
field goals made (755). She is second on
the career list for total points (1,862).
She also holds the record for rebounds in
a game (24) and blocked shots in a career
(259), season (77), and game (5). She
earned All-American from the
Association for Intercollegiate Athletics
for Women (AIAW) and All-Region IA
and All-New England honors in each of
her four years with the Rams. She served
as an assistant coach at her alma mater
after graduation.

THE 1982–1983 WRAMS BASKETBALL TEAM. The 1982–1983 WRams basketball team, from left to right, is as follows: (front row) Carol Smith and Helene Roher (co-captains); (middle row) Nancy Langham (head coach), Tracey Hathaway, Debbie Pereira, Tracey Turner, Sylvia DeCarr, Maureen Hogan, and Darlene Homondo; (back row) Naomi Graves (assistant coach), Jean Kelly, Ellen Quantmeyer, Mary Ann Icart, Barbara Miltner, Judy Ryan, Michelle Washington, Amy Staniszewski, Lisa Minich, Cathy Donas (assistant trainer), and Bob Schneck (assistant coach). Terri Calvert was not present. This team continued coach Nancy Langham's run of success and marked the start of the Michele Washington era. The five-foot ten-inch forward from Pennsylvania was named the Atlantic Ten Rookie of the Week three times and co-Rookie of the Year, and helped the Rams to a 19-12 record, the best in the school's history until 1996. This was only the start of a career that became the finest in WRam history. She and her fellow freshman teammate Ellen Quantmeyer provided the Rams with a remarkable one-two punch for four years.

MICHELLE WASHINGTON, SUPERSTAR.
"She had a fluidness and an agility that put her far above the rest of the field. . . . She established herself as a monument to URI women's basketball, personifying the dreams and goals of what the young program was about in the early 1980s." Beth James wrote these words for the 1996 WRam media guide. Michelle Washington (10) holds the records for most points in a game (35), a season (602), and a career (1,943). She leads the list for field goal percentage in a season (.543) and a career (.503). She is the recordholder for rebounds in a season (320), and a career (1,195). She is fourth in career blocks and second in steals, testament to her completeness as a player. She is one of two Rhode Island athletes (with Art Stephenson) to score 1,000 career points and grab 1,000 career rebounds. She was an AIAW All-American and a two-time Kodak District I All-American. The display case (left) in the Keaney Gym lobby shows her No. 10 and some of her awards.

ELLEN QUANTMEYER—THREE TIME HUSTLE AWARD WINNER. From 1982 to 1986, Michelle Washington and Ellen Quantmeyer (right) provided the best one-two punch in URI women's basketball history. Quantmeyer, a five-foot eleven-inch force under the boards, ranks third in career rebounding, with 911 caroms. She is 10th in all-time scoring (1,023 points) and fifth in field goal percentage. She complemented the elegant Washington with her tremendous hustle and defense. She won the team's Hustle Award three times and the Best Defensive Player honor twice.

COACH LINDA ZIEMKE COMES TO KINGSTON. From 1986 to 1989, the Rams fell on hard times, winning only nine games. In the spring of 1989, the university hired Linda Ziemke, who had been the head coach at American University, to rebuild the program. Ziemke led Rhody for 10 years, winning 106 games and losing 174. She achieved the ultimate goal—an NCAA bid with her 1995–1996 team, the university's first and only trip to the cherished national championship tournament.

THE 1995–1996 RAMS—BOUND FOR THE NCAA. Members of the most successful team in the annals of Rhode Island women's basketball strike a pose. From left to right, they are as follows: (front row) Lori Killingsworth, Jayme Yarger, Dayna Smith, Marcie Byrd, and Jennifer Worthington; (back row) Erin Fuller, Jaime Gray, Kerrie Giroux, Samantha Herrick, Martinique Alber, Sadie Bader, and Tasha King. They won 21 games and lost 8. They put together one five-game and two six-game winning streaks. They were 13 and 3 in the Atlantic 10, winning the East Division championship. In the first round of the NCAA, they faced powerhouse Oklahoma and pushed the Sooners right to the wire, losing 90-82. Six Rams earned individual accolades, either nationally or within the Atlantic 10. They played before the four largest crowds to watch Rhody women's basketball in Keaney Gym.

LET'S PLAY BALL! Warmups are over, the buzzer has sounded, and the Rams advance to the bench for the final huddle. Shown, from left to right, are Kerry Giroux, Marcie Byrd, Dayna Smith, Marty Alber, Jayme Yarger, and Jaime Gray.

HERE'S THE PLAN; LET'S GO GET 'EM! All hands on deck as the Rams get last-minute instructions from coach Linda Ziemke (center) before taking the floor. Joining in on the left are the three assistant coaches, Karen Sowada, Jessica Smith, and Erik Johnson.

TASHA KING, ALL-CONFERENCE FORWARD. Tasha King, a West Virginian, was an outstanding four-year player (1993–1997) for the Rams. In the 1995–1996 season, she led the team with a 17.4 scoring average and an 8.1 rebounding average. She was in the top five nationally in three-point shooting percentage (.420). She stands fourth in Rhode Island career scoring, with 1,151 points.

REBECCA BRIGHT, ALL-TIME RHODY GREAT. Rebecca Bright, a Vermonter, came to Kingston in 1991 and established herself as one of Rhody's greatest all-time players. She was a main reason that the Rams made such great progress in rebuilding, as they won 8, 11, 20, and 16 games in her four year stint. Remarkably, she finished third in all of the following career lists: points (1,665), scoring average (18.6), field goals (652), field goal percentage (.475), and free throws made (347). On January 2, 1995, she netted 37 points against Dartmouth to set a single game record.

NEED AN ASSIST? CALL ON DAYNA. Dayna Smith, a five-foot nine-inch guard from Pittsburgh, Pennsylvania, played for the Rams from 1992–1996. Her name appears in many record book categories, a testament to her all-around ability as a great impact player, but the numbers that catch the eye are under the heading of assists. She holds the single game record (16 at Temple University on January 23, 1995, the game shown above) and the season record (239 during the 1994–1995 season). It is the career record that is astounding: she dished out 793 assists during her four years in Kingston, more than double the second-place number of 370. While helping others to score, she was an excellent shooter as well, scoring 1,174 points, good for eighth on the all-time list. In addition, she is first in all-time three-point shooting, knocking down 184 shots. An excellent defender, she had 351 career steals, second on the all-time list. She was co-captain, with Marcie Byrd, of the most successful team in Rhode Island women's basketball history, the 1995–1996 squad that achieved Rhody's one and only trip to the NCAA Tournament.

KERRY GIROUX'S SENIOR NIGHT CELEBRATION. All of Rhode Island likes a local scholar-athlete, and Kerry Giroux of West Warwick proved to be a favorite during her four years at URI. Often used as the "sixth man," she was a great defender and ball hawk. Her contagious enthusiasm always gave her teammates and the crowd a lift. Her parents, Terry and Norman Giroux, join her on Senior Night, a tradition held before the last home game, honoring and thanking the seniors for their contributions to the URI women's program.

A MADDENING EXPERIENCE AT MARCH MADNESS. The URI women had to hope for an at-large bid to the NCAA Championship Tournament. Here, they experience the annual ritual of selection night on television to learn which 64 teams will be going to the Big Dance. The tension is thick as, from left to right, Kerry Giroux, Jayme Yarger (one row back), Dayna Smith, and assistant coach Jessica Smith wait hopefully for the University of Rhode Island to appear on the screen. With despair about to take over the room, URI was the 64th team named, resulting in much rejoicing. (Courtesy Providence Journal.)

DAYNA SMITH RETURNS AS ASSISTANT COACH. The 1997–1998 Rhode Island team was the beneficiary of a young assistant coach, Rhode Island's greatest point guard and recordholder for assists, Dayna Smith. Smith (right) stayed on through another year when she served part of the season as interim head coach. Here, she is giving some advice to the players.

THE 2001–2002 COACHING STAFF. Belinda (Boe) Pearman was hired to lead the Rams starting in 1999. In three seasons under her leadership, Rhody moved from 2 to 11 to 15 wins. She is flanked by her two assistants for the 2001–2002 season, Tom Garrick and Marc Wilson. Garrick, from West Warwick, was no stranger to URI, having starred at guard for the men's team from 1984–1988 as he helped lead the Rams to the NCAA Sweet Sixteen. He served as the assistant coach for the URI men's team for three seasons, from 1998 to 2001.

FROM WALK-ON TO ALL-CONFERENCE PLAYER. Yatar Kuyatch, born in Liberia, attended Mount Pleasant High School in Providence. She was a freshman walk-on in 1998 and established herself as an impact player. A business management major and dean's list student, she sparkled for the Rams as a fine shooter, rebounder, and leader. A two-time third-team all-conference selection, she scored 1,001 career points and picked off 607 rebounds.

WOMEN'S BASKETBALL—A COMMUNITY FAVORITE. A delegation from nearby Chariho High School roots for the Rams at a January 1996 game, shown on ESPN and won by Rhody over the University of Massachusetts 86-74. The growth of women's basketball has enriched not only the campus but also the greater–Rhode Island community. High school teams and coaches from all over the state have visited Keaney Gym to enjoy the action. Youth groups have met the players and received autographs at postgame receptions. The senior citizenry has embraced the players. The players and coaches have conducted community outreach programs. The future is bright for women's hoops at URI.

Six

THE ATLANTIC 10 YEARS
1982–2002

HANG OUT THE BANNER. The NCAA banner recognizing the 1987–1988 Rhode Island Rams' Sweet Sixteen achievement hangs in Keaney Gym under the golden ram proscenium. Following their trips to the NCAA (1978) and the NIT (1979 and 1981), Rhode Island's men's teams fell on a few lean years. In 1982, The Rams joined the newly formed Atlantic 10 Conference, along with other charter members Massachusetts, Rutgers, Temple, St. Joseph's, Penn State, Duquesne, St. Bonaventure, West Virginia, and George Washington. Brendan Malone, appointed head coach in 1984, had recruiting success but departed for the pro ranks after two seasons. He was replaced by Tom Penders, who led URI to a 1987 NIT appearance and a 1988 NCAA bid, along with a national ranking of 12 in one postseason poll. Penders also departed after two seasons, and his top assistant, Al Skinner, was appointed head coach in 1988.

COACH BRENDAN MALONE AND STAFF, 1984. Brendan Malone (third from left), an assistant coach at Syracuse, was named head coach in 1984. Shown with him are members of his staff, from left to right, Tim O'Shea, Al Skinner, and Jamie Campaglio. When Malone resigned in the fall of 1986 to accept an assistant's job with the New York Knicks, his successor, Tom Penders, kept the same assistants.

THE 1987–1988 TEAM. This 1987–1988 team photograph was taken on the shores of the Atlantic. These NCAA-bound Rams did the Ocean State proud, winning 28 games and losing only 7. The players, from left to right, are as follows: Bonzie Colson, Mergin Sina, Dennis Tabisz, Andre Green, David Bernsley, John Evans, Tom Garrick, Carlton "Silk" Owens, Josh Oppenheimer, Steve Lane, Jimmy Christian, Brian Jenkins, Kenny Green, and Jim Eitner. The coaches, from left to right, are assistant coach Al Skinner, assistant coach Rich Pagliuca, head coach Tom Penders, assistant coach Matt Brady, and assistant coach Jamie Campaglio.

SMOOTH AS "SILK." Brooklyn native Carlton "Silk" Owens arrived in Kingston in the fall of 1984 and played four seasons for the Rams. A real fan favorite, he played with a special flare and proved to be one of the finest point guards to ever wear the Keaney blue. His sleight-of-hand manner of delivering the ball to his teammates placed him first on the all-time assists list at the time, at 502. He was a remarkable scorer as well, netting a career total of 2,114 points, second all-time, and making him only one of two (Steve Chubin, the other) to have surpassed the 2,000 career mark . He is first in most points in a season, with 762 in 1987–1988. He holds the top all-time average (.462) for three-point field goal shooting. He teamed with backcourt mate Tom Garrick to lead the Rams to the Sweet Sixteen during March Madness of 1988.

FULFILLING A RHODE ISLANDER'S DREAM. Tom Garrick entered URI in the fall of 1984. A West Warwick native and great high school athlete, he had not been heavily recruited. Through his dedication and hard work, he established himself as a fine shooting guard and, along with Silk Owens, formed a formidable backcourt tandem that was one of the country's finest. Garrick's name is prominent in the record book. Among his greatest achievements are his all-time point total (1,573, 16th on the all-time list) and most points in a game (50 against Rutgers in the 1988 Atlantic 10 tournament, tying him with Tom Harrington for most points ever scored in a game). He is second in most points scored in a season, with 718 in 1987–1988. Garrick was also an excellent assist man, fourth on the all-time list, with 407. He went on to a successful five-year career in the NBA and eventually returned to his alma mater to coach.

GAME ONE OF MARCH MADNESS, 1988.
Rhode Island received an at-large bid to
the 1988 NCAA tournament and faced
highly regarded Missouri in the first round
at Chapel Hill, North Carolina. Rhody's
starting five—Tom Garrick, Silk Owens,
Mergin Sina, Bonzie Colson, and Johnny
Evans—all played well, and their sixth
man, Kenny Green—rebounder and shot
blocker superb—stifled many Tiger
attempts and sparked the Rams to an upset
win 87-80. Here, Garrick launches a
jumper as Evans and Green position
for a rebound.

GAME TWO OF MARCH MADNESS, 1988. Two days later Rhody's opponent was Syracuse
University, a perennial power and 1987 NCAA runner-up. Syracuse was led by All-Americans
Dennis Coleman and Sherman Douglas, and few gave the Rams any hope. However, Owens,
Garrick, and company had other ideas, and in a superbly played game, the Rams achieved upset
number two with a stunning 97-94 victory. The photograph shows Tom Garrick (22) hawking
Syracuse's point guard Sherman Douglas and Bonzie Colson shutting down Coleman (44).

RHODY FANS ARE THE GREATEST. March Madness yields wonderful human interest stories that entrance the nation. None could top the story represented by this photograph. The gentleman in the middle is Thomas Garrick Sr., father of Tom Garrick, Rhody's star co-captain and favorite son of West Warwick. Thomas Garrick Sr., blinded by a World War II explosion, married the nurse's aide who cared for him, and the couple raised a wonderful family. He attended all the Rhode Island games, and with the help of his portable radio and the guiding descriptions of a son or daughter next to him, he could hear and sense the action. This picture was taken during the Syracuse game in Chapel Hill, North Carolina. The joy of all reveals that the Rams are about to pull a major upset, propelling them to the Sweet Sixteen. Others pictured, from left to right, are as follows: (front row) Tom's sister Stacie, Tom's nephew Stace, and Tom's brother John; (back row) longtime Ram loyalists Bob Terino, Steve Koussa, Chris King (administrative assistant, men's basketball), Carl Koussa, and Ray Freitas (president of the Fast Break Club). The next stop for the Rhody faithful was to be the Meadowlands Arena in Secaucus, New Jersey.

How Sweet (Sixteen) It Is. Having dispatched both Missouri and Syracuse in the 1988 NCAA first two rounds and earning Rhody's first-ever trip to the Sweet Sixteen, the Cinderella Rams became one of the best stories of the tournament. Here, immediately after the Syracuse game, CBS television's Brent Musberger (left) and Billy Packard (right) interview, from left to right, coach Tom Penders, Silk Owens, and Tom Garrick.

Rhody the Ram Meets the Duke Blue Devil. Euphoria was in the air as the Rams returned to Kingston and began preparations for their round of the Sweet Sixteen match up with one of the tournament's top seeds, Duke University. The Eastern Regional finals were played in the Meadowlands Arena in Secaucus, New Jersey. Here, Rhody the Ram and Duke's Blue Devil exchange some pregame repartee.

SWEET SIXTEEN ACTION UNDER THE HOOP. Silk Owens (10) floats through Blue Devil traffic for two in NCAA Sweet Sixteen action. Duke's All-American Danny Ferry (35), Robert Brickey (21), and Billy King look to defend. The game was played with great intensity. Duke took an early lead, but Rhode Island gained the upper hand midway through the second half. Foul trouble hurt the Rams down the stretch and Duke prevailed, 73-72.

DANCING WITH THE DEVILS IN THE SWEET SIXTEEN. Kenny Green (24), seen here soaring for a rebound, was a key player for the Rams. His career numbers tell the story: 1,724 points (11th on the all-time list), 996 rebounds (fourth all-time), and 328 blocked shots (first all-time, far surpassing any other player). He was the premier shot blocker in the nation. He made eight blocks in a game, five different times. He blocked 124 balls during the 1989–1990 season, a Ram record. Remarkably, he did all this on two bad knees, which drastically limited his practice time.

AL SKINNER NAMED HEAD COACH. Following the 1988 NCAA, coach Tom Penders abruptly departed for the University of Texas. His top assistant, Al Skinner (center), was tapped to be the new coach. In nine seasons his characteristic reserve and dignity infused the Rams with stability and brought steady success to the program, including two NIT bids (1992 and 1997) and two NCAA bids (1993 and 1997). His teams had five wins and four losses in postseason games. Overall, he won 138 games and lost 126. He is flanked by his two assistants, Bill Coen (left) and Tim O'Shea.

HIGH-POWERED SCORER. Eric Leslie played three seasons for the Rams (1988–1991) and compiled a career 1,453 points, 22nd on the all-time list. In 1989–1990, he filled the nets for 645 points, a fifth-highest season total. A year later he averaged 23 points per game, sixth best in Rhody hoop history. Here, he floats under the basket for a twister against Duquesne University.

JEFF KENT, A POWER IN THE MIDDLE. Rhode Islander Jeff Kent played for the Rams from 1988 to 1992. Strong in the low post, Kent could also step out and shoot the three-pointer. Jeff is 35th in career points (1,231), 7th in rebounds (732), 6th in blocked shots (93), and 3rd in three-point shooting percentage (.407). His senior year he led the Rams to a 22-win season and an NIT tournament appearance that included a first-round win at Vanderbilt and a thrilling double-overtime victory at Boston College.

THE VICTORS MEET THE PRESS. The 1992–1993 Rams won 19 games and tied for the second spot in the Atlantic 10, earning an NCAA bid. They were matched against Big Ten power Purdue, whom they upset 74-68. Shown at the postgame press conference, from left to right, are Mike Moten, Rafael Solis, coach Al Skinner, and Andre Samuel. Rhody's next opponent was North Carolina, the eventual champion. The Rams were overwhelmed 112-67. During the game Carlos Cofield caused some smiles at the scorer's table when he asked if he could use the phone "to call 911."

THE 1993–1994 MEDIA GUIDE.
The caption is appropriate for these four URI players who always brought "a lot of game" to the way they played basketball. Andre Samuel (23) is 20th all-time scorer (1,490 points), Abdul Fox (25) is 36th on the list (1,224 points), and Carlos Cofield (11) is 34th (1,234 points). Kyle Ivey-Jones (50) had a uniquely explosive style as a jammer, a rebounder, and a shot blocker.

THE 50TH ANNIVERSARY. In December 1995, the 1945–1946 Rhode Island team was honored preceding the annual contest with Providence College. These 22 and 3 Rams captured the hearts of the basketball world with their thrilling performance in the 1946 NIT. Bill Woodward (left), author of *Keaney*, presides. Enjoying the proceedings, from left to right, are former players Bob Shea (hidden), Ernie Calverley, Al Nichols, Al Palmieri, and Ken Goodwin, Gov. Lincoln Almond, athletic director Ron Petro, and Ram Booster Club president Carl Koussa.

THE GREAT DANE. In the summer of 1993, a six-foot nine-inch 18-year-old from Denmark attended the World Scholar-Athlete Games held at the University of Rhode Island. Michael Andersen had been recruited by coach Al Skinner to play basketball for the Rams. He was short on experience, but Skinner saw potential. The result: Michael became a standout post player and rebounder for the Rams and helped lead them to the 1996 NIT and 1997 NCAA tournaments.

THE 1996–1997 SENIORS. These four members of the Class of 1997 helped the Rams to two postseason appearances. Pictured, from left to right, are Chad Thomas, Chris Wosencroft, Michael Andersen, and Ibn-Hashim Bakari. Ram fans will always remember Bakari's incredible career game against Temple in 1997 as one of the greatest individual performances in Ram hoop history. Bakari was unstoppable as he poured in 22 points from all over the floor, including all five three-point attempts, leading the Rams to a thrilling 85-82 victory.

MIDNIGHT MADNESS, OCTOBER 1997. The tradition of a spirited celebration for the first basketball practices for men and women excites these Rhody Rowdies as the 1997–1998 teams take the floor at midnight. A special highlight was the "California Cool" arrival of new head coach Jim Harrick by body-surfing down the stands with the help of students and hopping on a Harley-Davidson motorcycle to take a lap around the floor. Harrick had won a national title at UCLA.

THE TEMPLE RIVALRY. Perennial favorites in the Atlantic 10 and frequent NCAA qualifiers, Temple had won its first 23 contests with the Rams, starting back in the days of coach Frank Keaney. Al Skinner was able to do something about that. He defeated Temple the first time he played the team in 1989 and, in the 20 games Skinner coached against the legendary John Chaney, he won 9. Here, Tyson Wheeler dribbles against Pepe Sanchez in 1997, a winter in which the Rams beat the Owls three times, twice met in overtime.

RHODY SPIRIT ABOUNDS. The evolution of the cheerleading tradition has demanded increased athletic skills. Here, members of a URI squad from the mid-1990s display great strength and versatility as they entertain the crowd during a time-out. Pep bands, the Ramettes, and mascots have always inspired Rhody Spirit in support of Rams basketball.

"FOR WE'RE RHODE ISLAND BORN AND RHODE ISLAND BRED . . ." The Rhody Pep Band has always added a special ingredient to the spirited environment that is Runnin' Rams basketball. In addition to performing at games, the band plays at pep rallies, inside and outside arena lobbies, at alumni gatherings—wherever it can help infect people with Rhode Island basketball fever.

110

TYSON WHEELER—LITTLE MAN, BIG GAME. In 1994, Al Skinner's coaching staff did not have far to travel to find a point guard who would take over the floor leadership for the Rams for the next four years. New London, Connecticut, yielded Tyson Wheeler, a diminutive bundle of energy with a huge heart and infectious joy for the game. He had magical hands and would dazzle Ram fans with his deft ball handling and passing, while pouring in a career 1,918 points, third on the all-time list. A great three-point shooter, he made nine against St. Joseph's in 1998, the most ever in a URI game. He hit 91 three-pointers in 1997–1998, a single season record, and he is the career leader with a total of 302. He is Rhody's greatest assist man of all-time, holding the records for a single game (13), a season (205), and a career (712). He is the career leader for steals, with 205. He and Cuttino Mobley, his running mate at guard, formed one of the greatest backcourt tandems in Rhody hoops history. Here, Tyson (center) dishes a look-away pass against Temple as he leads a fast break. Running the floor on the left is Michael Andersen.

THE "CAT" SLAMS ONE HOME. Philadelphian Cuttino Mobley, the "Cat," arrived in Kingston in the fall of 1994. He eventually teamed with Tyson Wheeler to form a dream backcourt duo, one of the finest in the nation. Mobley was a lithe six-foot four-inch slasher who played the game with great passion and contagious enthusiasm, which rubbed off on his teammates and fans alike. Blessed with remarkable athletic ability, he was a great leaper for his size, ran the floor with abandon, and had a sweet touch from three-point range. His competitive fire made him a natural leader. Though he played only three seasons, he scored 1,334 career points, tied for 30th on the all-time list. He is 4th on the all-time 3-point list, with 146, and has the best free throw percentage in a career, at .821. Mobley played brilliantly his senior year, helping to lead the Rams to the NCAA and an eventual spot in the Elite Eight. He was named the Atlantic 10 Player of the Year, the only Ram to ever be so recognized. Now in his fourth year of a successful NBA career, he led the Houston Rockets in scoring for the 2001–2002 season.

REYNOLDS-DEAN SOARS AGAINST UMASS. Coach Al Skinner's recruiting philosophy, which seemed to lean away from big names and toward those with potential to grow, was well illustrated by this young man from Georgia, who was attracted to Kingston in the fall of 1995. His name is Antonio Reynolds-Dean, and his game was blue-collar, lunchpail, hard-nosed. He measured six feet five inches tall, but he played well above his height. In his four-year career, he became Rhody's 15th leading scorer, accumulating 1,576 points, practically all from "down low in the paint," many as put-back rebounds, and most in traffic against taller opponents. He snared 1,028 rebounds, third highest in Ram history. He was what basketball aficionados refer to as a warrior. In 1997, coach Al Skinner left for Boston College, and Jim Harrick, former Pepperdine and UCLA coach, took over the Rams for the 1997–1998 season, which proved to be one of Rhody's finest. In this photograph, Reynolds-Dean (34) goes up against the Massachusetts Minutemen in a critical February 1998 game played in Amherst, a game won by the Rams in double overtime 87-85. The win catapulted them to a strong finish and helped assure the coveted NCAA bid.

113

SENIOR NIGHT FOR THE 1998 RAMS. The last 1997–1998 home game was played against Fordham on February 28th. It was time to say thanks, but not good-bye, to four Rhody stalwarts, from left to right, Tyson Wheeler, Cuttino Mobley, John Bennett, and Joshua King (not shown). A standing-room-only crowd packed Keaney Gym, which was standard for all home games during this magical season. Still to be played were the Atlantic 10 and NCAA tournaments.

FIRST-ROUND NCAA ACTION, 1998. It was time for March Madness. The Rams received an eighth seed in the Midwest bracket and drew Murray State (Kentucky), champs of the Ohio Valley Conference, as their first-round opponent. The game was played in Oklahoma City. The Rams were ready to play and, with a great display of speed and balance, disposed of their foe 97-74. Here, Luther Clay (35), the Rams' powerful center, grabs a rebound against the Racers. (Courtesy Providence Journal.)

SECOND-ROUND NCAA ACTION, 1998.
URI faced the nation's number one team
and tournament favorite, the University
of Kansas Jayhawks, who were led by two
All-Americans, Paul Pierce and Raef
LaFrentz. The Rams played one of their
greatest games ever. With minutes left in
the seesaw battle, they put on a burst and
grabbed the lead for good to win the game
80-75. Every Ram played a major role,
including Joshua King, seen here
grabbing a loose ball. (Courtesy
Providence Journal.)

MORE SECOND-ROUND ACTION. Rhode Island's valuable "seventh man" was David
Arigbabu, a junior from Germany. He was a backup player for the front court starters. Here, he
goes up for a shot against Kansas All-American Raef LaFrentz. The Ram defense was
outstanding against the Jayhawks, consistently frustrating LaFrentz and Paul Pierce. At the
buzzer delirious fans rushed the court to greet their heroes, and a large midnight crowd awaited
the team's return at Green Airport.

A RAM SEND-OFF BY RHODE ISLAND'S FIRST COUPLE. Rhody spirit gripped the Kingston campus as the team prepared for its Sweet Sixteen appearance in St. Louis. Arrangements were made for three charter flights to carry 1,000 Ram supporters to the Gateway City. The opponent was to be Valparaiso of Indiana. A huge send-off pep rally was held in the Memorial Student Union. Pictured here as the team bus departs are two URI alumni, Marilyn Almond, Class of 1958, and Gov. Lincoln Almond, Class of 1959.

SHOTGUN GOES TO THE SWEET SIXTEEN. A secondary mascot was added to the URI spirit arsenal in 1996. The head of the Rhody Spirit Committee rescued a stuffed cow literally from the scrap heap. He named her Shotgun and saw to it that she was present at all sorts of social and athletic events. During games the students enjoyed tossing her about like a beachball. Here, Shotgun is safely strapped into her seat on a chartered flight to St. Louis for the Sweet Sixteen.

THIRD-ROUND NCAA ACTION, 1988. Before 22,172 fans in St. Louis's Kiel Auditorium, URI faced Valparaiso, another Cinderella team with an eye on the NCAA Elite Eight. Valpo had upset Mississippi and Florida State to advance. Luther Clay (35) slams one home as the Rams took the lead before half time. (Courtesy Providence Journal.)

MORE THIRD-ROUND ACTION. Antonio Reynolds-Dean (34) goes high to slap away a Valpo attempted shot as Tyson Wheeler (21) and Luther Clay (left) prepare to get the offense rolling. The Rams held off the stubborn Crusaders in a hard-fought second half and captured the victory 74-68. (Courtesy Providence Journal.)

CUTTINO BREAKS DOWN VALPO. This photograph shows Valparaiso's attempt to double-team Atlantic 10 Player of the Year Cuttino Mobley. Ever alert to open teammates, the Cat dishes a quick pass that lead to an easy Ram basket. (Courtesy Providence Journal.)

TYSON SALUTES THE CROWD. The win over Valpo sent the Rams to the fourth round of the 1998 NCAA, referred to as the Elite Eight. Stanford had beaten Purdue earlier in the evening, so the match-up was set: the Rhode Island Rams versus the Stanford Cardinals, to advance to the Final Four. Here, Tyson Wheeler with his big smile acknowledges the crescendo of cheers pouring down from Ram fans as he leaves the court following URI's exciting victory over the Crusaders.(Courtesy Providence Journal.)

RHODY VERSUS STANFORD FOR THE FINAL FOUR. In a game for the ages, played before a standing-room-only crowd in Kiel Auditorium on March 22, 1998, the Rhode Island Rams battled the Stanford University Cardinals, ranked in the top five during most of the season. The prize was a trip to the Final Four in San Antonio. Here, Preston Murphy, Rhody's fine guard and sixth man extraordinaire, drives against the Cardinals. In the game Stanford seemed to have the upper hand early, but Rhody fought valiantly and gained the lead by as many as 12 points midway in the second half. As Stanford pecked away, the Rams led by 4, with 26 seconds left. Stanford stunned Rhody with two quick three-point plays—layups followed by foul shots—and took the lead. There was chaos during the final seconds, and Stanford prevailed 79-77, inflicting a heartbreaking loss on the men in Keaney blue. Hundreds of Rhody fans, filled with pride for their team's amazing run, embraced their heroes at a postgame reception. (Courtesy Providence Journal.)

THE 1997–1998 RHODE ISLAND RAMS. When coach Al Skinner left URI's helm in April 1997, he left the cupboard full of excellent players for his successor, Jim Harrick. The predominantly junior-senior team accomplished a 21-7 regular season record and a 25 and 9 overall mark. After their remarkable run to the NCAA Elite Eight, national polls ranked them as high as 10th in the nation. Team members, from left to right, are as follows: (front row) coach Jim Harrick, Preston Murphy, Joshua King, Cuttino Mobley, Tyson Wheeler, John Bennett, Antonio Reynolds-Dean, and assistant coach Larry Farmer; (top row) Sarah Tuzinski (manager), Maureico Gay, Luther Clay, Andrew Wafula, David Arigbabu, Tory Jefferson, and Brand Daniel (manager). Missing are assistant coaches Jerry DeGregorio and Tom Penders Jr. (Photograph by David Silverman.)

MCDONALD AND KAULL MAKE THE CALL. When Jim Norman retired in 1995 as the "Voice of the Rams," Steve McDonald (right) became the new play-by-play announcer for Rams Radio. Here he chats with color analyst Don Kaull, a standout Ram of the 1960s. In addition to game duties, McDonald hosts the Rhode Island coach's Show and the Rams Radio call-in show. He also is a fixture as master of ceremonies at URI athletic banquets and other ceremonial functions.

LAMAR ODOM—RARE TALENT. The 1998–1999 Rams were strengthened by the addition of Lamar Odom. A remarkably versatile player at six feet ten inches tall, he was an excellent rebounder, shot blocker, and shooter from anywhere on the floor. Perhaps his greatest gift was his deft passing ability. The season's highlight moment came at the buzzer in the Atlantic 10 Tournament final against Temple when Lamar hit a 25-foot buzzer-beater for a 62-59 win, giving the Rams their first Atlantic 10 title and their fourth NCAA bid in the 1990s.

THE 1999–2000 COACHING STAFF.
Following the 1998–1999 season, Lamar Odom left the the NBA, and coach Jim Harrick left for the University of Georgia. Rhode Island replaced Harrick with assistant coach Jerry DeGregorio, who went on the lead the Rams for two seasons. DeGregorio (right) solicits advice from his two assistants Tom Garrick (left) and Jeff Jones.

THE NEW ARENA CAMPAIGN A SUCCESS. October 21, 2000, marked a major day in the history of URI basketball. The success of a campaign for a new convocation center led to this day's groundbreaking ceremony. Friends of Rhody basketball gathered in Keaney Gym for introductions and a game of hoops among the prime movers of the campaign. From left to right are alumni Brad Boss, Alan Zartarian, Tom Ryan (campaign cochair), Phil Kydd, and Frank Feraco. (Photograph by Nora Lewis.)

BREAKING GROUND. Following the Keaney Gym festivities, it was time to put the spades in the earth. Doing the honors, from left to right, are Bob Beagle (vice-president for University Advancement), William Holland (commissioner of Higher Education), Cathy Ryan, Tom Ryan (campaign cochair), Robert Carothers (URI president), Marilyn Almond, Lincoln Almond (governor and campaign cochair), and Sally Dowling (Board of Governors chair).

JIM BARON NAMED HEAD COACH. In the spring of 2001, Jim Baron was named the new head coach of URI men's basketball. His rebuilding efforts in his initial season at the helm clearly revealed a dedicated work ethic and an improved team chemistry that helped his young Rams win eight games, including the last regular season game against his former team, St. Bonaventure, an 80-72 upset victory and the last game ever played in Keaney Gym.

TOM RYAN, GRACIOUS BENEFACTOR. The new $54 million arena is named the Ryan Convocation Center, and appropriately so. Tom Ryan, Class of 1975, is the chief executive officer of CVS. He served as cochair of the Convocation Center campaign. His vision and generosity helped make the new building a reality. On site, Ryan (left) and URI president Robert Carothers contemplate the center's exciting future. (Photograph by Nora Lewis.)

A NIGHT OF NOSTALGIA IN KEANEY GYM. The last game ever played in Keaney Gym was on March 2, 2002. To start the evening, students, faculty, and alumni were invited to participate in a basketball toss. A half-mile line was formed from Lippitt Hall, the Rams' first home on the quadrangle, to Rodman Hall, their second home, and finally to Keaney Gym. URI athletic director Ron Petro awaits the ball as it nears the Keaney Gym entrance. (Photograph by Nora Lewis.)

A CEREMONIAL JUMP BALL. Before the final game in Keaney Gym, a ceremonial jump ball was conducted at center court. The invited dignitaries suited up in a variety of Ram jerseys, worn throughout the 49-year history of the facility. Many participated. Pictured here, from left to right, are the following: Tracee Hathaway Luster (former player), William Holland (commissioner of Higher Education), Tom Ryan (alumnus and cochair of the campaign for the new arena), Jim Keaney (grandson of coach Frank Keaney, for whom the building was named), Gov. Lincoln Almond, Marcus Evans (current player, with headband), and Tom Carmody (former men's coach). (Photograph by Nora Lewis.)

CUTTING DOWN THE KEANEY NETS. Vedrana Bajagic, a senior from Yugoslavia, does the honors as she cuts down the nets in Keaney Gym, symbolically ending 49 years of Rhody basketball history on this grand old "home court advantage." As Ram all-time great Tom Garrick said, "I loved playing here. When we took the floor, we knew we could win." Such was the sentiment of all former Rams who had played in this "grand old barn." (Photograph by Nora Lewis.)

SAYING GOOD-BYE TO AN OLD FRIEND. The crowd at the last game in Keaney Gym gathers on the floor following the Rams exciting 80-72 win over St. Bonaventure to pose for the final photograph. The scoreboard shows the date, and the victorious Rhode Island team stands in

front with coach Jim Baron to bid farewell. During the building's 49-year history, the Rams enjoyed their friendly confines to the tune of 336 wins and 175 losses. (Photograph by Nora Lewis.)

RHODY BASKETBALL ARRIVES AT A NEW HOME. After posing for the crowd picture, Rams fans lined up shoulder to shoulder along both sides of the lengthy corridor connecting Keaney Gym with the new arena for the final ball toss. Frank Keaney's grandchildren, Jimmy and Barbara Keaney, backed by coach Jim Baron and his team, receive the ball and deliver it to the Runnin' Rams new home. (Photograph by Nora Lewis.)

THE THOMAS M. RYAN CONVOCATION CENTER. This state-of-the-art facility becomes the crown jewel of the university campus. As a center for athletic and cultural events, entertainment, conferences, and major university gatherings, it is the sparkling new home for URI basketball, with a seating capacity of 8,000. On basketball's opening night in November 2002, the Thomas M. Ryan Convocation Center launches another 100 years of Runnin' Rams excitement, which will continue to enrich campus and community life.